ZOMBIE-FIED

How Voters Turned Into
Shuffling Zombies
and Other Rants from a Senior Citizen

by M.A. Wyner

This book represents the opinions and commentary of M.A. Wyner. She can be reached at

Mawyner@sc.rr.com

All rights reserved.

This book, or parts thereof, may not be reproduced in any form without permission.

Copyright ©2016 by M.A. Wyner

Library of Congress Catalog Number: 2016943608

ISBN 978-0-9888683-8-0

Published June 2016

Printed in the United States of America

http://www.facebook.com/wawyner

When you have made evil the means of survival, do not expect men to remain good. Do not expect them to stay moral and lose their lives for the purpose of becoming the fodder of the immoral. Do not expect them to produce, when production is punished and looting rewarded. Do not ask, 'Who is destroying the world?' You are.

— Ayn Rand

PREFACE

A number of years ago I was perusing the Obituaries in our local paper. For some reason, once you hit a certain age, the Obits seem more interesting than the comics. I had often wondered why Mom found them so fascinating. She said (old joke) that she wanted to see if she was mentioned. But actually she was looking for anyone she knew.

So back to the past. My gaze fell on one entry that was at least three long columns in length. Who on earth was this guy? How important was he? Imagine my surprise when it read as though the deceased had written it himself, one of those *in the event of my death, place this in my obit.* He spent most of the three columns railing against a certain president, how the policies and actions were going to give him a heart attack; and if he did die, it was because of said president.

I am guilty of writing a number of letters to the editor in my past, many weren't published but a few were. Today, I'm not sure three columns would do it. Hence, I sat down and wrote ZOMBIE-FIED. If that poor guy had taken the time to write a book, let it all out, ease his conscience, unburden his soul, his heart might not have been under so much stress.

In my teens, politics didn't interest me. Even in my late twenties I hadn't bothered to register to vote. Once I did,

I fell into the old female cliché … I voted for whichever guy was cutest. If I had been old enough, I would have voted for Kennedy, either one, but not the one who couldn't maneuver a car over a bridge. Dad loved the peanut farmer. I read the guy was a nuclear scientist, or some such thing. So he's smart. He'd probably do a good job. Wrong! Reagan? Who's going to vote for an actor? Well, he was a governor, so he had that going for him; and he ended up surprising most everyone.

I finally did get a grasp of this politics stuff. Guess as you get older, start to earn a paycheck, and see how much the government is sucking out of it, you start to pay closer attention. Always thought I had a high tolerance level; but when I think back to the guy with the three-column obituary, I didn't want to wait until the stress got to be too much to unleash my rants. Don't get me wrong, I do offer some common sense solutions to a number of issues. The more I type, the more issues pop into my head. Too many subjects…too little time.

So without further ado…

READING, WRITING, AND …

What on earth is happening to our educational system? Whatever happened to reading, writing, math, English, science, history, and a bit of the arts (music, theater, etc.) thrown in? And let's not forget about gym. Why are there so many non-essential classes taking up precious time? I recall reading in our local paper of grade schoolers spending a couple hours outdoors playing Frisbee. At least they were getting exercise, but it wasn't part of gym. This was an energy company promoting an environmental cause by passing out "green" Frisbees. Want to teach kids about the environment, green energy, eating vegan, saving the planet? Save it for an after school class and make it voluntary.

Poor kids. Like little zombie Stepford kids, they do and say what they are taught. I'm sure teachers want to teach the subject they studied in college. That's where their passions lie. They didn't sign up to do the job of parenting or bouncer or to read pages and pages of edicts from higher ups regarding the *cause du jour*. Students need to learn the basics, prepare for college or a profession. This way, if they focus on the basics, they won't have to retake high school English in college. The only extra class I would toss in is finance. Students need to learn how to save for the future rather than rely only on Social Security.

Which brings us to …

COLLEGE

Critical thinking? (That's a great buzz phrase colleges like to use.) Let's face it. If a kid hasn't learned how to think before entering college, he needs to go back to high school. The scary question is, are they thinking for themselves? They have spent eight hours a day for twelve years among certain teachers struggling to pass on thoughts and ideology dictated by the government and are now handed off to a college for four or more years of even more ideological persuasions, majority of which bend way far to the left. They may call it critical thinking, but it's more like teaching students to think like their left-leaning professors. Shouldn't it be illegal for a student to be graded based on whether the student agrees with the professor? Matter of fact, shouldn't teachers/professors be required to keep their political leanings to themselves?

Tuitions are through the roof, but they don't have to be. I have a novel idea. Why not require students to only attend classes that benefit their choice of major? If they plan to be engineers, they should only attend classes pertaining to their chosen profession. Why should there be requirements that the student take other classes which have nothing whatsoever to do with their major?

The Daily Caller had a list in August 21, 2015 of some of the dumbest college courses. These include classes on

Being Bored, Wasting Time on the Internet, How to Win a Beauty Pageant, Stupidity (at a cost of over $63,000!), The Sociology of Miley Cyrus (over $62,000!). And let's not forget the college in Utah with their annual Sex Week workshop to learn all about bondage, domination, sadism, masochism, and the list goes on and on and on. Mom... Dad, did you realize you were paying for such drivel?

While we are at it, let's do away with the keggers and drinking on campuses. Bet colleges love the fact that students drink their way through the first year, thus forcing parents to pay for five years of college rather than four. If we outlaw the drinking and only have students take classes pertinent to their major, they should be able to zip through college in three, if not two-and-a-half years.

As if that's not enough to worry about, now student activists are taking over the asylums, making demands on firing professors who don't bow to their agenda, requiring the creation of specific departments to make sure the universities adhere to their wishes. One university is going so far as to spend $1 million on an audit of their diversity programs. Really? Are students there to learn or cause trouble? Should we shutter all of the colleges until students understand that their parents are paying huge sums for them to get an education and that there is no such thing as a degree in activism?

Now I read students at Yale are demanding the university

remove the requirement that they read "only white male authors." Instead, they want to "focus on literature relating to gender, race, sexuality, ableism, and ethnicity." One question: What the heck is ableism?

In one way I agree with students as it relates to a point I made above. If you aren't going for a degree in English Literature, forget about studying these dead poets. Subjects that have nothing to do with a degree should NOT be required.

Just saying.

ADVERTISING

Prescription drugs were never advertised on television when I was growing up. I'd see the usual non-prescription aspirin commercial, but not until maybe the last decade have I seen the airwaves inundated with prescriptions for anxiety, high cholesterol, restless leg syndrome, blood pressure, the list goes on and on. It used to be drug companies only communicated with doctors and then the doctors discussed treatments with the patients. Now, like kids seeing a new cereal advertised while watching Saturday cartoons, adults imagine every pain and ailment affiliated with every drug commercial, then head off to the physician to see if they can add one more bottle to the collection in their medicine cabinet.

And who can forget erectile dysfunction? Are there really that many guys who can't rise to the occasion? And why are the wives in these commercials so much younger than the husbands? Isn't there a point in life where you just enjoy golf, shopping, finding new restaurants, and traveling?

I bet those water filtration plants work on overdrive, filtering out all the drugs and over-the-counter supplements people put into their bodies. I know, I know. Some people need certain medications. However, deaths due to overuse of prescription drugs is through the roof. And we haven't even touched on the illegal drug use. I must have lived a very sheltered life, or Mom put the fear of the wooden spoon in me. I never had a desire to try drugs let alone smoke a cigarette. Didn't take my first sip of alcohol until I was almost legal age. Rarely hear about Ritalin anymore but it is still being used worldwide. Guess we have traded the wooden spoon for a few pills. How's that working out for society? There comes an age when kids outgrow their antsyness. Are there studies on long-term effects? Are scientists too busy studying how shrimp run on treadmills that they can't focus on the mental health of our kids?

Which brings us to …

WAR ON DRUGS

So many wars…so little time. How much money have we dumped into the war on drugs and how has that worked out for us? What I can't figure out is man's desire to separate from reality. One addict when asked why he couldn't/didn't stop his drug of choice said, "Think of your greatest orgasm...then multiply it by a thousand." Well color me flabbergasted. Hard to beat that!

Drug dealers say as long as there's a market for it, they'll keep selling. And I'm not just talking about the homeless guy shooting up in an alley (and exactly where does a homeless guy/girl get the money to buy the drugs? Oh, I forget. Their habit is a disability and they receive money from the government who thinks said addicts are buying food for themselves and their kids.) That white powdery stuff is floating around the board rooms, the chic nightclubs, and rich societies. "I worked for my money. I'll spend it however the hell I want!" Then we wring our hands and mourn the death of a celebrity who died too soon.

It's been many years since Nancy Reagan proclaimed, "Just say no." Perhaps they thought she meant to say no to heroin but bring on the prescription drugs. According to the Centers for Disease Control and Prevention, *Overdose deaths involving prescription opioids have quadrupled since 1999. From 1999 to 2014, more than 165,000 people have died in the U.S. from overdoses related to prescription opioids...In 2014 alone, more than 14,000 people died from overdoses involving prescription opioids.*

Some of the drugs most common in these deaths are methadone, oxycodone, and hydrocodone. Society has tried more rehabilitation facilities, incarceration, drugs to help them come down from dependency.

The U.S. and New Zealand are the only countries that allow direct-to-consumer advertising by drug companies. Why can't Congress order the Food and Drug Administration to prevent all drug companies from using direct to consumer advertising? Kids and teens are getting into the parents' Xanax, Ritalin, hydrocodone, and god knows what else. If the government is serious about reining in the abuse of prescription drugs, they need to take action.

Experts now label addiction as a disease, just like they do alcoholism. All this does is qualify the addict for, again, disability benefits so they have money to buy more of their drug/drink of choice. They can dress it up with any word they want. They all have one thing in common, the cranky me says. Lack of self control.

Hey, I understand. It took me years to conquer my addiction. The only way I succeeded is that they took away access to my comfort food—Salerno Chocolate Covered Graham Crackers.

Yes, those squares of a delicious blend of graham and chocolate were sold in the downstairs bakery at our local Goldblatt's store. The store sold lunchmeat, candy, and cookies downstairs. All of the clothes, toys, and household items were located on the other floors, all accessible by a rickety elevator with the old time grated door and controlled by a pleasant employee who had a mean cane he used to control the number of shoppers climbing onboard.

The lady behind the cookie counter told me they made them there. I was a bloodshot raging lunatic when I learned the store was closing. I rushed to the basement to hoard as many pounds of chocolate covered graham crackers that I could, only to see them ripping open the Salerno packages. At first I was upset that the woman had lied to me. Goldblatts didn't make their own cookies. But the addict in me realized I could now buy them at my local store.

I was in heaven. There was nothing better after dinner than a cup of hot tea and four cookies. The hot tea slowly melted the chocolate blending those fantastic flavors. Then something unseen happened—Salerno ceased making those wonderful cookies. Do I picket their offices? Lead a write-in campaign? Boycott all their other products? No. I decided there were similar cookies on the store shelves made by other companies. That would suffice.

But it didn't. The chocolate coating tasted like plastic wrap. The graham crackers were smaller with the texture of cardboard. I tried them all. Although I didn't curl up in a fetal position in the corner of my room or see strange animals floating in the corners as I went through withdrawal, it was a jolt to my system. My comfort food was no longer available so I had to put my big girl panties on and deal with it.

I know, my addiction isn't anything like what true addicts go through. My point is that it is all self control. If a celebrity is caught cheating on his wife, he cries sex addiction and checks into a swanky resort. Porn addiction, video games, the Internet, cell phones, texting, smoking, Fantasy Football. You name it, there are a number of things people will do to isolate themselves from the real world.

So what's a Society to do?

Let's see, China certainly found a way to get their citizens off drugs during the Opium Wars. They just dragged the addict out into the street and shot him in the head. How's that for a deterrent? Singapore gives the addicts two chances at rehab. They keep them in rehab so long that eventually the drug dealers have fewer customers. However, if the addict relapses after his two stints in rehab, off he goes to prison. Course, here in the U.S., that's a great place to get more drugs.

I know, not the way a civilized society acts. Bet you would be surprised to learn that during the prohibition era our own government poisoned tens of thousands of people by poisoning the alcohol. Making liquor illegal didn't work. People made their own or bought it on the black market (after all, it was the Capone era!). So a new formula for denaturing industrial-grade alcohol was proposed by anti-drinking forces in the government. One senator called it legalized murder. Three drinks and a person could go blind. Then scores of fatalities started to occur.

Thankfully, we are a bit more civilized today, but is that a good thing? We coddle them, sit them down in a room to talk about their mommy issues, give them a disability check. When will we ever learn? Libertarians believe people should be free to do anything, including drugs. They feel addicts are only hurting themselves. Wrong. The spouse suffers, the kids suffer, other family members who have to pitch in to take care of the children suffer. Society suffers because the addict isn't contributing, isn't reaching his or her full potential, and is a drain on government resources necessary to help those who actually need it. Society needs to stop glorifying drug use and start stigmatizing it. Terrorists in the Middle East have a bumper crop of drugs which funds their terrorist acts. And that's what has to stop. We need users to realize that their use fuels the drug wars and fuels terrorist acts. I know, they are too zonked out to care about bumper crops in the Middle East. So let's cut off the flow. Put more agents on the border. Returning veterans need jobs and they certainly know how to patrol and use a gun. Let's not forget about the homemade drugs. Such clever amateur chemists whipping up a bunch of meth in their garage or in your friendly, neighborhood trailer park. Really? You can't find a better way to spend your free time?

Which brings us to …

LEGALIZING MARIJUANA

How many years did it take society to demonize smoking? Bad for your health. Second hand smoke. Smoking sections in restaurants and on planes gave way to banning smoking in these places altogether. So what's with the pot? Isn't that smoking? Matter of fact, it has the most nauseating and disgusting smell that is fifty times worse than cigarette smoke. Smoking is smoking. I can understand medical marijuana, but I read the effect is only felt for the duration that you are smoking. So does that mean you light one after the other? And if you can only smoke in your house, not out in public (are you listening San Francisco?), what happens if you live in an apartment building? When I lived in an apartment I could smell everyone's cooking every single night. The stench from pot would be too much, not to mention if someone has kids in the building. Talk about second hand smoke! Who regulates the dispensaries? Who checks these doctors who hand out prescriptions for pot for headaches? A hangnail? Depression? Hell, who isn't depressed these days?

According to Colorado's crime statistics, the crime rate had dropped 32% from 2004 to 2012. Then starting in 2012 it rose 21 percent. What was the difference? Pot was legalized in 2013. For all those animal lovers out there, I heard on the radio this morning that veterinarians in Colorado are reporting that more and more pets are being brought in, high from pot. Seems pets are eating the marijuana butts they find on the ground. Abandon a puppy on the side of the road and you're charged with cruelty to animals. Get him high on drugs, oh well!

POLITICS

Why can't we be more like England? They allow a maximum of $30 million to be spent on campaigns. Here in the U.S., we spend more than that just on raising money for an election. In 2008 our candidates spent $1.7 billion. We could have supported four third world countries on the amount of money political parties have spent over the years. Better than that, we might have been able to put a dent in the deficit. The other nice thing about England is they can only start campaigning six weeks before an election. And here? A year and a half! Do the political parties really think we are paying attention eighteen months prior to election day? In the U.K. there is a ban on paid radio and television advertising on matters of *political or industrial controversy*. Ahhhh, wouldn't it be nice not to be barraged by campaign commercials?

The question of the President's birth certificate was a controversy that could have been avoided. For one thing, we shouldn't have to question a candidate's citizenship. Should we take someone's word for it? I guess we can assume honesty. But actually, by dragging it out, POTUS made the doubters sound hysterical and biased. Ingenious political move out of the Saul Alinsky handbook. I don't know about you, but when we moved and had to obtain new driver's licenses, we had to bring our birth certificates and proof of marriage. All of our important papers were in a safety deposit box. Why did POTUS have to wait for a hospital in Hawaii to come up with the paperwork? Unless one is delivered by a mid-wife, everyone is issued a birth certificate and should keep it handy. Am I wrong? That's a controversy that could have ended in five minutes but it dragged on and on.

What was more important to me was the lack of vetting by the media. Other than a book or two penned by the President, even the media didn't have much to go on. The problem was, they didn't care. I admit, I was caught up with the young man who gave that wonderful speech at the 2004 Democrat Convention. "… there's not a liberal America and a conservative America; there's the United States of America." What soaring rhetoric. But I soon forgot the speaker until the campaign of 2007. Then all of a sudden the name popped out at me. This was a community activist who made sure people had a voice in elections, made sure everyone registered to vote. But when he ran for Illinois State Senate, the old Chicago politics was at play… somehow the voting petition signatures of his challengers were invalidated, denying them a position on the ballot. Thus Obama was able to run unopposed. Then, when he ran for the U.S. senate, he was losing badly to Jack Ryan, a Kennedy-esque, smart politician. Soon the details of Ryan's *sealed* divorce records were splashed on the front page of the *Chicago Tribune*. (What part of *sealed* do we not get?) Ryan dropped out prompting the Republicans to put in a weak candidate, Alan Keyes, and Obama romped to a victory. Sure, politics is ugly. Sure, politicians get down in the mud. But why do they have to? It certainly doesn't bode well for the character of the man (or woman) if they have to resort to such underhanded tactics. Weren't we all hoping this new voice would add civility to politics? However, I do vaguely remember in campaigning that he told his followers, "if they bring a knife, you bring a gun." That certainly set the tone!

And then there was Bill Ayers, Reverend Wright, non-existent college papers. How is it we haven't heard of one former girlfriend or any reminiscing from former college classmates? I guess some faction of the country was vetting the candidate. But it certainly wasn't the majority of the media. Were we that eager to show the world how far we have come that we elect the first black president no matter his background? If we were that anxious to pat ourselves on the back, why not elect a Native American to the highest office?

This reminds me of an episode of *The Twilight Zone,* Season 3, Episode 24, *To Serve Man*. Aliens visited earth with great promises. They would end famine, wars, and create a virtual Garden of Eden. To prove their intentions, they added nitrate to soil in arid countries so everything would grow, ending famine. They built invisibility walls impenetrable by bombs thus ending wars. The media jumped on the bandwagon with headlines of *Aliens Offer Peace and Prosperity*. A few people were skeptical of their motives. But the aliens claimed the elimination of hunger, war, and suffering would be enough of a reward. Countries were able to disband their military, disarm their people. The aliens boasted about their own planet where it was always 76 degrees and the sun never set, fantastic free shopping. They offered trips to their planet and a continual line of people signed up and flew off to paradise. Then someone interpreted the book the aliens had left—*To Serve Man.* It was a cookbook.

Sound familiar? "We will fundamentally change America," our Commander in Chief said while campaigning. And people climbed onto that Hope and Change space ship in droves. Now we are sitting back and realizing our goose is cooked.

And we segue to…

ELECTIONS

Here's the elephant in the room...or donkey. Some like to brag that Democrats won the popular vote in five of the last six presidential elections. If you believe that, I have a bridge to nowhere to sell you. The numbers may confirm this but common sense doesn't. The majority of the country is center right. Has been for years, although now I believe Independents are creeping up in the polls. Common sense says the popular vote should reflect that. For those who don't know or remember, our elections are based on the Electoral College, not the popular vote where there is a higher chance of vote rigging — dead people voting, people voting more than once, voting in more than one state. In one election the opposing candidate didn't receive one vote in a county even though there are registered Republicans. In another election, there were more votes than registered voters. Voter fraud runs rampant, no matter how much the other side rails against voter I.D. laws. A couple elections ago when a group was trying to get as many people registered to vote as possible, there were a lot of Mickey and Minnie Mouse names on those applications. With over 200 million registered voters, everyone should be concerned about the integrity of the system.

Which brings us to the 2016 election. The average age of the three leading candidates is what? 70? 72? With all of the men and women over the age of 35 in this country, this is the best we can do? I want someone young and vibrant, full of new ideas. I don't want to see some tired, worn out, gray-haired person up at the podium. Maybe distinguished silver at the temples. Now I'll be accused of age discrimination but so be it. Yes, Reagan was old, so was George H. But they didn't look haggard. Then again, we got someone young, vibrant, and full of new ideas in 2008. How is that working out? I personally believed our 2012 candidates were the best hope we had. Unfortunately, the media and the political machine kept the blood pumping into the zombie voters. Can't blame it all on the glassy eyed shufflers. Many of the one-issue voters stayed home. If you want to win, you have to get off your duffs.

Side Note: It doesn't take much to doom a candidacy. Michael Dukakis practically swallowed up by a helmet while riding a tank. Howard Dean's infamous scream. Rick Lazio invading Hillary Clinton's personal space during a senatorial debate. Today, supporters appear to shrug at all of the blunders and liabilities of the two party nominees. Have we ever in our history had two worse candidates?

Another problem I see with voters is they rely on emotions. They did it in 2008. It was a great feeling—hope and change—those collective pats on the back with electing our first black president. Afterwards, even some news pundits admitted they knew very little about the guy. No vetting here, just a feel good moment. The entire world was captivated, even bestowing the Nobel Peace prize on someone who was barely in office long enough to get the first dusting of the Oval Office. People were voting against Bush, not for something.

Today, emotions run high against the political system and getting the shaft by entrenched politicians. They want an outsider, someone to shake things up. Doesn't matter that he ridicules and belittles his opponents. His followers eat it up. They are sick of political correctness, executive orders, and back room deals. Actually, aren't we all? How will those voters feel, though, after six months? One year? Four years? A little buyer's remorse? They don't realize that there is more at stake here than their pissed off feelings. There's the Supreme Court, the Senate, the House of Representatives which holds the purse strings. When emotions get in the way, no matter what it concerns, it rarely ends well.

Can't forget the ugliness of politics. People are sick of the name calling and misleading attack ads. One side is adept at labeling the opposition. Compassionate Conservative. Never liked that term. It implies that there are conservatives who aren't compassionate at all. Do we say fiscally responsible liberal? I'm sure there must be one or two Democrats who would like to see a balanced budget. What's with all of these terms and sayings to pigeonhole people? I believe there may be another Saul Alinsky quote in there… demonize your enemy. War on women…racist…bigot… homophobe…Islamophobe…etc. etc. Is this what has been fueling the vitriol aimed from both sides of the fence? The violence and threats hurled at rallies? My senior citizen gut tells me someone is pulling the strings from behind the curtain. Who would want our political system turned upside down? Who would want to sow the seeds of distrust, rage, and resentment among our citizens? Whom does it benefit if we turn into a third world uncivilized society eating its own?

Just asking.

Believe me, I understand the frustrations of voters. We have been left to feel like the ugly step-child. The government gives work permits to foreign college graduates while American graduates are struggling in low paying jobs. The country is $20 trillion in debt with no end in sight. Spending continues to outpace revenue yet all Washington wants to do is spend more. We had close to a $1 trillion stimulus and stimulated nothing. One of our Sentinel spy drones just happened to fly into Iran in 2011, completely unscathed, fully intact. Might have had a red bow wrapped around it. Then I read that a Hellfire missile which was headed to Europe for training purposes mistakenly made a detour to Cuba. Another gift, I presume, wrapped in a bow.

Does the wayward missile seem like a peace offering at a time when POTUS wanted closer ties with Cuba? Couldn't we have just bought a few boxes of Cuban cigars? And whatever happened to the transparency we were promised? Then there's all those new regulations—17,000 pages added in just five years. Schools are focusing on Common Core and bathroom assignments while our kids can't read and aren't prepared for college much less life. Parents are working two jobs and not getting ahead. Illegal immigrants receive benefits you and I can't get. Their kids get free or much lower college tuition. This Administration recently secured millions of dollars for summer jobs for refugees, NOT for American students. Fifty million people now on food stamps. Schools and towns are ill-prepared for the influx of kids, with or without parents, crossing the border. Sanctuary cities. The disastrous *Affordable* (really?) Health Care program. Skids of money missing in Iraq and Afghanistan. Forty-three million dollars spent to build a gas station in Afghanistan. Money taken from NASA's budget and used to fund Muslim Outreach Programs. The VA hospitals in disarray leaving our wounded veterans waiting months for treatment. Millions given to other countries, for what? To play nice with others?

For the first time in my adult life I am shopping at Big Lots and the Dollar Store. Not that I was used to shopping at Whole Foods and Ethan Allen and not that there is anything wrong with Big Lots and the Dollar Store. It just goes to show that things are nowhere near as good as this Administration wants you to believe.

So, yes, I understand voter frustration. But if we make the same mistake, if we aren't thinking with our heads when we vote, where will that leave this once great country?

God help us all.

People vote in one of four ways, in my very humble opinion.

Custom: People vote the way their parents always voted. They would never deviate no matter the issues.

Herd (zombie) Mentality: Just like there's peer pressure in schools, friends and neighbors influence a person's way of thinking, or try to. Can't forget the spouse either. Certainly don't want the husband voting one way and the wife another. In which case, they would cancel each other out and just stay home. Colleges (professors and fellow students) have cornered the market on brain washing…I mean critical thinking. If you have any doubts, just look at the number of times a conservative speaker is protested or uninvited to be a guest speaker. Freedom of speech on your local street corner but not in the halls of higher education. Look at how many college students are backing the candidate promising free stuff.

One Issue Voter: Maybe it's late term abortion (abortion is legal but we have been getting into gray areas. One side wants abortion on demand, the other wants zero abortion, while others want limits), a specific social issue, or one party isn't for unions and you've always been a union person so will never vote for said party. No one party will agree with every position you have. It's not a reason to sit at home, not when there are so many other important issues at stake.

Now the biggie…

The Media: How can anyone think there isn't a media bias? Reputable journalists have written about it. With the amount of time people spend in front of their television sets, computer screens, and cell phones, not to mention print material, voters are absorbing all kinds of opinions. Election ads, whether truthful or slanted, can influence a voter's opinion of a candidate. The smart voter will check out the accusations for accuracy. Others don't care, tweeting and posting whatever rumors they read or hear.

I don't have a magic answer on how to get voters to the polls. Would I trust allowing people to vote online? Not in a million years. Can't show a voter registration card through the Internet nor verify who is pushing the buttons (which is why I don't care much for absentee voting, except for the military). Can't have them vote when they renew their driver's license. Even if everyone's license expired every four years, it would clog the DMV, and we all know how slow they are on a good day. And it wouldn't get the votes in for the off-year elections. Withhold benefits? That's a thought. IF, and that's a big if, we could get the state computers to talk across state lines and verify when someone has voted, every person who did not vote would have their Social Security, disability check, food stamps, housing allowance, income tax refund, or some other benefit or payment, withheld until the next election cycle. Hit them in the wallet. If they don't receive a refund, aren't eligible yet for Social Security, or some other excuse, freeze their credit card(s).

It's *tough love*, but aren't we getting sick of *anything goes*?

In some countries they walk barefoot through a hot desert to vote. In the U.S., we are lucky if 50% of registered voters get to the polls during a general election. Off year elections are much worse. By sitting at home, our politicians are not being elected by the majority of the country. In most elections, a president is elected by 51% to 60% of those who bother to go to the polls. This means only 26% to 30% of registered voters are electing our president so the winner doesn't really have the backing of the majority of the country. No mandate. For those still confused by Common Core, I will use the math skills I was taught. We have 230 million registered voters. If only 120 million bother to vote and the winner receives 65 million votes versus his opponent's 55 million votes, that means our new president won with 54% of the votes. (65 divided by 120) HOWEVER, in reality only 28% of the country (registered voters) voted for him (65 divided by 230). Don't see how any president could be shocked when he receives major pushback on his legislation when 72% of the country didn't like his positions and policies.

Just a bit of reality check.

CLIMATE CHANGE
(aka Global Warming aka Whatever)

Where to start. There's a road about fifteen miles south of Lake Michigan called Ridge Road. According to *Calumet Beginnings*, by Kenneth J. Schoon, a former middle and high school science teacher and an active member in the Historical Community of Northwest Indiana, it's called Ridge Road because the number of glaciers over time pushed the land up, creating a ridge. You did catch the important phrase—*a NUMBER of glaciers*. There weren't gas guzzling SUVs back then nor six billion people on the planet.

Another great book, *Dark Winter—How the Sun is Causing a 30-Year Cold Spell* by John L. Casey, President of the Space and Science Research Corporation, explains the influence of the sun's spots on our climate, power grid, earthquakes, and even volcanos. I spent the last Earth Day reading this informative book. When the press and powers that be continually fill the airwaves with endless sky-is-falling, humans will be the death of the planet apocalyptic predictions, I knew there had to be other opinions out there. When the powers that be say "97% of scientists agree…" regarding man-made climate change, exactly how many scientists did they poll? Was it 97 out of 100 who work off of government grants? I read it's 97% of "published scientists." Many scientists with an opposing view are blacklisted from having their articles published. How convenient that those with an opposing view can't get published in the science magazines. They have to write books instead. One French meteorologist was fired for having an opposing view. Why do we condemn doctors (rightly so), whose research on drugs falls favorably on the side of the very same drug companies paying for the research, yet we are *expected* to believe climate scientists whose research is paid by the very same governments who tout the man-made climate change mythology?

Let's face it. The so-called experts lost their credibility years ago. First, there was data manipulation, polar bear cubs used in fake videos, computer models which only spit out information based on what man inputs. Then we have Al Gore's movie, *An Incomplete Truth*, which was so riddled with errors that in Britain they pulled the movie out of schools. Just changing the term from *Global Warming* to *Climate Change* sent up a red flag. They had to manipulate the term to fit their agenda. But really, don't we have more important things to worry about?

According to the Center for Disease Control, 2.5 billion people lack access to improved sanitation. Many of the tropical diseases come from poor sanitation. Every 90 seconds a child dies from a water-related disease. According to the U.N. Commission on Human Rights, there are close to one hundred million people worldwide who are homeless. Between the tilt of the earth's axis, El Nino, weather cycles, sun spots, solar flares, deep sea fissures, tectonic plates, sink holes, etc., is man really that arrogant that he can play God? There are so many other important, manageable issues where we should be focusing our attention and funding.

What we need to do is separate pollution from climate change. One we can control, the other is completely out of our hands. We are standing on a cooling ball of molten iron spinning at 1,000 miles per hour, circling the sun at 67,000 miles per hour. Our entire solar system is being pulled through the universe at a million miles per hour by what and to where no one knows, according to the late Carl Sagan. And we are worried that we might have hot summers and cold winters? Wasn't it just in 2008 that world scientists predicted the arctic would be completely melted by the end of that year? But in 2015, a ship carrying scientists to the Antarctic to study the melting polar cap got caught in the ice and had to be rescued.

Can we control the tilting of the earth's axis? The moon's magnetic force? How about volcanos which spew more CO_2 into the air than man ever could, not to mention the multitude of volcanoes on the ocean floors which belch not only CO_2 but also methane and other poisonous gases? If an earthquake is powerful enough, it can permanently shorten the length of Earth's day by moving the spin of the Earth's axis. The 2011 earthquake in Japan cut 1.8 microseconds off of our days. The Sumatra earthquake in 2004 knocked off 6.8 microseconds. Doesn't sound like much, but a second here, a second there, pretty soon there will be 360 days in a year. What about Mount Tambora? It boasts the largest eruption in history in 1815. Located in Indonesia, the eruption dropped the average temperatures five degrees and is known as the *year without a summer*. Crops failed worldwide. It disrupted weather patterns until 1888, not to mention the high amounts of sulfur dioxide spewed into the stratosphere. Does man think he can control Nature's unpredictable forces?

All we want to hear is a little fact-checking. A couple years ago it was reported that the National Oceanic and Atmospheric Administration fiddled with temperature data.

The media spits out other cute tidbits:

Climate change affects the earth's spin!

Seas will rise 15 feet! Florida will disappear!

While the doomsayers fill us with fear, there are other opinions out there which receive hardly a footnote:

FROM THE UTAH GEOLOGICAL WEBSITE

Currently, we are in a warm interglacial that began about 11,000 years ago. The last period of glaciation, which is often informally called the "Ice Age," peaked about 20,000 years ago. At that time, the world was on average probably about 10°F (5°C) colder than today, and locally as much as 40°F (22°C) colder.

What causes an ice age and glacial-interglacial cycles?
One significant trigger in initiating ice ages is the changing positions of Earth's ever-moving continents, which affect ocean and atmospheric circulation patterns. When plate-tectonic movement causes continents to be arranged such that warm water flow from the equator to the poles is blocked or reduced, ice sheets may arise and set another ice age in motion.

Do ice ages come and go slowly or rapidly?
Glacials and interglacials occur in fairly regular repeated cycles. The timing is governed to a large degree by predictable cyclic changes in Earth's orbit, which affect the amount of sunlight reaching different parts of Earth's surface. The three orbital variations are: (1) changes in Earth's orbit around the Sun (eccentricity), (2) shifts in the tilt of Earth's axis (obliquity), and (3) the wobbling motion of Earth's axis (precession).

FROM THE FARMER'S ALMANAC WEBSITE

Sunspots *are magnetic storms on the surface of the Sun.*

Solar flares *are strong flashes of x-rays and light energy* *that shoot off of the Sun's surface into space at the speed of light.*

Coronal mass ejections *(CMEs) are massive clouds of gas and magnetic matter that are eruptions spreading into space.*

*Other solar events include **solar wind streams** that come from the coronal holes on the Sun and **solar energetic particles** that are primarily released by CMEs.*

Damage to 21st-century satellites and other high-tech systems *in space can be caused by an active Sun which generates geomagnetic storms. Even in inactive solar cycles, the Sun emits large solar flares—which could cause billions of dollars in damage to the world's high-tech infrastructure—from GPS navigation to power grids to air travel to financial services.*

Radiation hazards for astronauts and satellites *can be caused by a quiet Sun. Weak solar winds allow more galactic cosmic rays into the inner solar system.*

Global climate change *including long-term periods of global cold, rainfall, drought, and other weather shifts may also be influenced by solar cycle activity.*

The solar minimum *occurred in 2008 and 2009; during those two years, there were almost NO sunspots, a very* *unusual situation that had not happened for almost a century. Due to the weak solar activity, galactic cosmic rays were at record levels.*

Solar Maximum: *The Sun's record-breaking sleep ended in 2010. In 2011, sunspot counts jumped up. In February of 2012, the sunpot numbers reached a peak of 66.9.*

In late 2013, NASA reported, 'The Sun's global magnetic field is about to reverse polarity.' The sunspot number climbed into the 70s. This is still very low. By February of 2014, sunspots averaged 102.8 spots a day, which is the first time the cycle broke 100.

In April, 2014, the sunspot number peaked a second time, reaching 81.9. This is likely the solar maximum. Many cycles are double peaked, however, this is the first time the second peak was larger than the first peak (in February, 2012).

This sky is falling mentality has been going on for decades, and there have been a lot of predictions. But how many of the following have come true?

Civilization will end.

Close to 200 million people every year will starve to death.

Global famine will reduce world population by 2000.

World population figures are closing in on 7 billion. Instead of starving, the world has an obesity problem. Matter of fact, one doomsayer claimed mass famines would be the demise of England by 1980!

We will all be wearing gas masks to survive air pollution.

This was predicted to start in 1980. Have you seen the air in China? They don't do much to clean up their air and their citizens do wear masks, but that's far from everyone. We've made great strides in reducing air pollution, but to the point of predictions made in 1985 that half of the sunlight wouldn't be able to reach Earth? Really? And these are college-education scientists? One doomsayer went so far as to suggest mandatory birth control. I believe China tried that.

The world will run out of crude oil by the year 2000.

Hmmmmm…it's 2016 and the wells are still pumping.

Now the latest…

The *doomsayers* have new proof of our annihilation. They have just discovered five islands that have vanished in the Pacific proving the dramatic impact of climate change on rising shorelines.

Sounds threatening.

However…

Last year an underwater volcano CREATED a new island in the South Pacific. (See above on the subject of shifting tectonic plates.) Mother Nature taketh away, and Mother Nature giveth!

Whether it's alar on apples, save the planet, horned owls, toads, baby turtles, environment ad nauseum, people looking for a cause bigger than themselves flock like zombie moths to the flame. Sure, I think baby owls are cute. Nature is also smart. Remove trees and the owls find another tree. Yes, baby seals are worth saving from an oil spill. Who didn't have a good laugh, I mean who wasn't shocked, when do-gooders released the clean baby seal into the ocean only to watch a whale swim up and eat it?

Good intentions are not always the best intentions.

Let's be honest: No one knows what will happen. Yes, we all want clean air and clean water. If the earth decides to tilt a couple degrees in either direction, there isn't much we can do about it. If the sun decides to become hotter (and just where is the thermometer they use to measure that?!), we may have to build shelters underground. If the sun decides to cool a few degrees, just buy another coat. (Maybe Mother Nature knows it's going to cool which is why there seems to be an epidemic of obesity.) Global warming, global cooling, the sky is falling, yada yada. We need to worry about our outdated power grid. One good solar flare and we'll all be reading by candlelight.

Unfortunately, some people don't like those who question man-made climate change. There's talk of taking some type of legal action against deniers. Can we say communism? Since when does a free society punish people for having a different opinion?

And then there's hypocrisy. How much pollution is caused by all the jets flying to a climate summit? What about all the SUVs to get those attendees from point A to point B? Has no one ever heard of GO TO MEETING DOT COM?

ENERGY

Unintended consequences. Why is it the powers that be never look at the unintended consequences? According to the ***Wildlife Society Bulletin,*** 573,000 birds, which includes raptors and bats, are killed every year by wind turbines. What about ethanol? More unintended consequences. Corn prices went through the roof. Besides, fuel is needed to run the equipment used to harvest the corn. We have vast amounts of coal and oil. Other nations are ramping up the construction of nuclear power plants.

Sun, wind, and hydroelectric are the answer, according to some. Unintended consequences. Humans can live for only three days without water. How much of the water will be depleted? Guess you could say it's renewable if we catch rain water. What if it doesn't rain? What do people living in deserts do? Alaska, Iceland, other northernmost countries don't have sun all twelve months of the year. And I don't think wind turbines would work very well at 40 below temps.

It's impossible to make a wind turbine without those other pesky fuels. We need to make the steel and concrete. The blades are made of fiberglass, and petrochemicals are used to make fiberglass. And the steel? That's the stuff that starts with iron ore dug out of the ground by heavy equipment also made of steel and running on fuel, transported by a ship powered by diesel fuel when it's coming from a foreign country, then onto a steel mill…you get the picture. And let's not forget the concrete for the base of the turbines. The equipment to make the concrete is powered by coal or natural gas. Even the production of concrete produces CO_2.

Our benevolent Administration gave $120 million in grants to advance solar energy. Isn't there a solar generating system in the Mojave Desert which produces twice as much carbon emissions as power plants who are forced into cap and trade programs? The increased carbon emissions are the result of the plant's use of natural gas as a supplemental fuel. Just like with the wind turbines, you still need some type of supplemental fuel. Unintended consequences.

All of this yakking is just to show how we cannot get away from using fossil fuels. Just getting people to acknowledge that we can never be strictly green would be progress. Can we call those who won't acknowledge that fact, fossil deniers?

Just asking!

Geothermal energy. I was shocked to read that China, Kenya, Philippines, El Salvador, Italy, Iceland, Mexico, Japan, and New Zealand all are tops at producing geothermal energy. But which country is Numero Uno? The United States. Double shocker. So where are we using it? How expensive is it? And exactly how warm can my house be in the winter and how cool in the summer? I have to warn you, my husband likes it around 76 degrees in the winter and 74 in the summer. I hear geothermal heat might get your house to a max of around 50-60 degrees, which is why most of the geothermal heating in the U.S. is in the warm, western states. Seems to me, with all that molten ore deep in the earth that we should be able to tap into something a little hotter to raise those household temps. Course, what kind of toxic elements would we be tapping into? What kind of non-renewable energies would be needed to pipe deep into the earth? And exactly how expensive would it be? Inquiring minds want to know. I'm flexible and open to suggestions. Will solar panels allow me to watch TV plus run the dishwasher and washing machine at the same time? I have visions of that actor who pedals a stationary bike in his kitchen to run his toaster. Good for him, but not for me. Guess we are spoiled.

Some environmentalists would probably love to see us heat our houses with wood. Oh wait. That would kill the trees, and I read somewhere that it gives off more carcinogens than a cigarette. I recall several years ago some brainstorming environmentalists thought we should use diapers instead of toilet paper in order to conserve trees. Unintended consequences. We would use more electricity, soap, and water to wash those things. I don't think they thought that idiotic idea through completely. You can't make this stuff up!

Which segues to the environment...

According to Reclaimed Enterprises, 2016, as of 2009 we had 1,908 landfills. It decreased from 7,683 in 1985. On the negative side, some cities have done away with landfills and prefer to ship their garbage to another state. However, garbage sent by truck or train generates that icky carbon dioxide stuff. So what do we do?

Incinerators! Yes, those bastions of noxious odors that used to fill the air when I was a kid. But today they are far cleaner, using dozens of filters to remove all the icky stuff. Denmark has been using garbage as a fuel source for years. It has cut down their energy costs, reduced the use of landfills. Matter of fact, they claim the plants run so cleanly that there are more pollutants emitted from fireplaces and barbecue grills.

Denmark isn't the only country with this waste-to-energy concept. There are now over 400 plants across Europe. To be fair, we do have some in the U.S. (the EPA must have been asleep at the switch!) but the number pales in comparison to Europe. Cities still send their trash to distant landfills. Pretty soon, we will run out of space, or they will be trucking the stuff from New York City to some vast plain in Wyoming, wasting energy hauling the trash by truck. We might think those landowners would never sell their land. But then we do have that wonderful phrase, *imminent domain*!

Naysayers are afraid people will no longer recycle. (Really?

That's an excuse?) Some still look at incinerators as dirty. Wonder what they think of all the bodies being cremated. Clean incinerators have to be a lot better than a landfill covered over with dirt and grass that emit that horrible methane smell. Have the environmentalists not discovered the dastardly deeds happening in Europe yet? Things change so quickly. Perhaps the *greenies* are chaining themselves to the incinerator doors as we speak!

Just saying.

RELIGION

Lutheran, Presbyterian, Methodist, Mormon, Catholic, 7th Day Adventist, etc. etc. According to Wikipedia, there are close to 4,200 different religions in the world. What's a God to do? At the end of times, does he put all the names in a cookie jar and draw out the winning religion? Instead of Fantasy Football, maybe God has Fantasy Religion.

I remember questioning Sister Mary Margaret in Sunday School:

Me at 8 years old: "Sister, if God knows all things, then why didn't he stop Jimmy's dad from driving his car into a light pole?"

Sister MM: "Well, he can't be all places at once."

Me: "If Adam and Eve were the first people God created, and there wasn't anyone else around, how could God expect them to marry before eating the 'forbidden fruit'?"

Cricket sounds

Me: "Why did God create poisonous snakes, bees that sting, bugs that make us sick, and illnesses that kill us?"

Sister MM: "Of course God didn't create those; the Devil did."

Me: "If God created us in his image, does that mean he's jealous, greedy, a thief, hateful, spiteful…"

Sister MM: "Of course not. It just means we all have goodness in us, just like God."

Me: "But why does ……?"

Sister MM: "Everyone turn to Page eight. We are going to learn a new hymn."

I expected Father Nathaniel to step in to explain that God gave us the ability to choose right from wrong. Naturally, no one knows the answers. The adult M.A. is just as confused as the eight-year-old M.A. You see opposing teams praying for victory yet only one wins. Does that mean God likes one team better than the other? Or did God flip a coin?

The *Twilight Zone* fan in me says God worked his butt off for seven days, then moved on to the next solar system, giving us a book on behavior and a sense of right and wrong, with each person left to discover his or her own talents and capabilities, after instilling in (some of) us the ability to find cures and invent things to make our lives a little better.

And speaking of this book on behavior, the teenage M.A. had all kinds of questions for Sister Mary Margaret (I obviously couldn't get out of her Sunday School class). The Bible wasn't written until 40 years after the death of

Jesus. Who on earth remembers what they said or heard 40 years ago? I can't even remember what I ate last week. And what ever happened to the God of the Old Testament? I think there are a number of groups that deserve a bit of smoting, burning bushes, and turning of bodies into stone these days. Sister Mary Margaret always said bad people will answer to God at the end of time. Well, excuse me for being impatient, but bad people can do a lot of destruction before the end of time.

We learned early on that praying was private, something you do in church or the privacy of your home. To this day, it gives me a hinkey feeling when I see people holding hands and praying over their meals in a public place. A cashier at a local store said, "have a blessed day" when I checked out. Double hinkey. Our Founding Fathers had it right about separation of church and state. But I would toss "public" in there, too. It's one thing if the Pope wants to hold a public mass in Central Park. I'd consider it an *open-air* church. Come-to-Jesus moments on a street corner or my front stoop by a Bible-toting convert? Uhhhh….no. What religion a person wants to follow, is up to him. Politicians, on the other hand, should try not to wear their cross on their sleeves. Some are so heavy into theology that voters are turned off for fear his election means mandatory church attendance and the branding of red letters on women's foreheads should they break some Commandment.

However…

Can the powers that be please outlaw cults? Sure, I guess any organized whatever can exist, but it makes you wonder what attracts people to certain *cults*. Followers of the Heaven's Gate religious cult were waiting for the space ship hidden in the comet. (Can't seem to wrap my head around that one.) There are many others, some huge AND receiving tax exempt status. A cult leader with twelve kids and five common law wives, each receiving government Aid to Dependent Children just isn't right. Shouldn't there be some type of litmus test before granting a *fad* organization tax exempt status?

Speaking of which —

TAXES

Federal, state, income, social security, Medicare, sales, estate, corporate, motor vehicle, vehicle stickers, schools, toll roads, gas tax at the pump…does your wallet feel empty yet? The 16th Amendment gives the federal government the power to tax, and the 10th Amendment gives the states the power to impose taxes. Naturally, each state and even city and county can impose what they want. I lived in a city which charged a fee when you sold your house. Some local taxes need to first be approved by the voters at the ballot box. Too bad we can't do the same for federal taxes.

The highest tax rate was 90% under Eisenhower with Carter close behind at 70%. Under Ronald Reagan the top rate was 28%. Now one presidential candidate wants 90 percent of our money. Good luck with that. His supporters think that's wonderful, because they think he means everyone but them. The problem with our tax system isn't that the rich aren't paying enough. The problem is that not everyone pays. Half of the country pays zip. Not only do they pay nothing, they get money back via earned income credit, child credits, lifetime learning credit, adoption credit, elderly and disable credit, etc. etc.

Before I'm slapped with the customary cold-hearted label, I do agree that some credits are justified. But for even the lowest of income earners not to pay something, is inconceivable. Even if it's a meager five percent. Eventually each person will need some service, whether police, fire, military protection, you name it. As some people say— "everyone should have skin in the game." And are there really religions that claim their members do NOT have to pay taxes because it's against their tenets? Are we really going to let that pass the smell test? And why are people and corporations allowed to hide their money in off shore accounts?

In 2014 the government collected $3.021 trillion in revenue. However, spending was $3.504 trillion. How soon until the bill collectors knocked on your door if you ran your household budget that way? What is so hard about realizing you can't spend more than you have? Better question: How does the government run without a budget?

Federal revenue in 2015 is estimated at $3.18 trillion. Federal spending for 2015 was $4 trillion. How's that for Common Core math?

So what's a government to do? Flat tax is the answer. Lower incomes, say up to $40,000, would pay a flat 5 percent. Everyone else would pay, say, a flat 15 percent. Corporations should enjoy paying less than corporations in other countries. However, with corporations making huge profits, should we control what the executives make? We are a capitalist country. The government shouldn't dictate what the owners or top tier people make. But they also shouldn't pay crappy wages while the big shots drive BMWs, and CEOs who, if they do a crappy job, are fired and given an eight figure golden parachute. Where's the fairness in that? I suggest one way to remedy the situation is that whatever bonus is paid to the big shots, an equal bonus has to be paid to each worker. Course, the smart execs will just raise the salaries of the top tier and not pay bonuses. What next? Power of the purse? Consumers don't buy their products or don't use their services? I'm certainly not for raising minimum wages to ridiculous amounts. After all, before the slow economy we have now, only entry level, like high school age workers, took the jobs at the burger joint or retail store. Now people with degrees are stuck in these jobs because they can't find a good paying job in the field for which they paid tens of thousands of dollars to obtain a college degree. Yet we are told the economy is great, humming right along. Brain washing. We are subjected to endless mantras of "the economy is good, everything is great, you are feeling sleepy…" I don't know about you, but I certainly know it isn't good.

Which brings us to…

PORK SPENDING

Why is it some politicians wouldn't cut spending to save their souls? They are all worried about backlash from their constituents. But why? I would think more highly of my congressmen if they told me how much they cut in spending.

Senator Tom Coburn wrote a series of books on the ridiculous pork spending. His latest book reveals luxury houses for temporary border patrol agents, taxpayer funded grants to give a Disney resort a makeover (at $100 a day ticket per person to attend DW, they need a grant to do renovations?), price gouging (why do we have to overpay for parts and other equipment? Doesn't the government look for the lowest bidder?), and so much more that my head hurts just reading it. Course, my favorite is studying shrimp on treadmills. Scientists claim all these research grants are for the good, but IMHO they just want the money to keep flowing.

Now that Senator Coburn is retiring, he is passing on the torch to an Oklahoma representative. However, Senator Jeff Flake of Missouri came out with a doozy: *Wastebook—The Farce Awakens, A Report on Wasteful Government Spending, starring Monkeys on Treadmills, Parties for Hipsters, and Sheep in Microgravity, featuring Party Buses, Winemaking for Minors, the Science of Beer Koozies, Zombies in the Whitehouse, Life-Size Pac Man, Dating Secrets for the*

Unattractive and dozens more. Can anyone in Washington justify this waste of taxpayer dollars? Makes for interesting reading because the title only mentions a few; and I haven't even touched on the money we give to other countries to play nice or all the pallets of missing money during the wars in Iraq and Afghanistan.

This news flash caught my eye. There was a gender and glaciers study by researchers at the University of Oregon that cost a bundle of our money. This much-needed research studied the *'feminist political ecology and feminist postcolonial' approach when researching glaciers and climate change.*

Not quite sure what all that entailed or what it all means. One press release quoted a professor that the report, "... noted how women are more vulnerable to glacier changes and hazards than are men."

I'm on a roll now…

How's this for money well spent? The National Science Foundation spent $600,000 of grant (taxpayer) money to study — you won't believe this — why people cheat on their taxes. This is 2016 and this study won't be completed until 2018. Lots of cheating can occur before the study ends.

And this isn't the only study made. In the past thirty years there have been more than a dozen studies. Close to

$350,000 was spent in 1988. Also included were a study on auditing and the effects on penalties. In 2009, $137,000 was spent studying tax evasion and corruption around the world. Then in 2010 behavioral responses to tax enforcement was the target at a cost of $243,000. How about I do the study for half the amount — people cheat because they can. Study completed and it only took me thirty seconds!

Course, the IRS will say they don't have enough employees to catch all the cheaters. For one thing, we could start with all of the IRS computers talking to each other. Someone can file a fake return in more than one state but unless the state computers talk to each other, the culprits will never be caught.

People have complained to Congress about the *jack booted thug* techniques sometimes used by the IRS. It's obvious the IRS doesn't know how to identify the real cheaters from those making honest mistakes. And unless they make the penalties for the cheaters severe enough, they will just keep doing it. (A flat tax right off the top would solved these problems.)

I'm not done yet —

The National Institutes of Health spent more than $80,000 to study whether mice stutter. For one thing, I didn't know mice talk. I stuttered as a kid. I was a nervous Nellie, OCD, you name it. Maybe there's something here I'm not grasping. Maybe there's some hormone in their little pink tongues that, in some way, relates to human speech patterns. All I see is money down a rat…mouse…hole.

Do we need to create a Waste Department? Are lengthy bills passed so quickly, not one person has the time to read what is being added? How about shortening these bills and take out all of the legalese? These grants are a way of making a congressperson's constituents feel like they are doing something. But are the constituents paying attention as to exactly where their tax dollars are going?

And while they waste money on these frivolous items, the government is running on outdated computer systems, some that are 50 years old. We aren't talking about the receptionist's laptop. These dinosaurs are in the Defense Department, Treasury, Social Security (no wonder it took them two years to correct an error in my account!), Medicare, Transportation Department, and some of these systems still use floppy disks. And when the Veterans Department claimed thousands of veterans were deceased, and thus their benefits cancelled, was this because of antiquated computers? Human error? Or just plain incompetence?

And while I'm at it, why do committee hearings cost money? I hear of complaints on the billions spent on the Benghazi hearings. Why? Naïve me thought that's part of congressional members' job description. They sit on committees and have hearings when necessary. Are they getting an extra paycheck for being on a committee? Why?

And why does a first lady, ANY first lady, need 20 or 25 assistants? Maximum of five. Any more than that and they pay for them out of their own pocket. All these parties are doing is paying back contributors by employing their friends and/or family.

Once a president leaves office, why is he still given secret service protection? Not only do we have to pay the salaries of this protection, but oftentimes the government (taxpayers) are billed for the monthly rent and the building of a place nearby to house the secret service. Former presidents used to receive lifetime protection until 1997 when it was changed to a limit of ten years. I might go along with that, although five years is better. But our current occupant of the White House in 2013 changed it back to lifetime for both him and the First Lady. And Congress went along with this spending. With the current POTUS *retiring* soon, that will be five presidents and their wives who will be receiving lifetime protection at taxpayer expense.

Ex-presidents are no longer in the limelight so nix the protection. Is there really a need for that many secret service on the golf course? Won't that hold up play?

Just asking.

WAR ON POVERTY

It was President Lyndon Johnson in 1964 who enacted the program to end poverty. Wonderful program. Today, not one person is homeless, hungry, or jobless. Matter of fact, everyone is in the upper middle class or higher.

Wait…wishful thinking.

Truth is, after more than 50 years and $22 trillion (yes, that's with a "t" and this does NOT include Social Security and Medicare), we have more homeless, hungry, and jobless. Johnson's Great Society campaign included federal aid, food stamps, housing, healthcare, education, money to build more schools, homes, libraries, hospitals, job training for the jobless, etc. etc. He threw everything at it not knowing what would work. Sound familiar? Sounds like the $800 billion stimulus with shovel ready jobs that were never shovel ready. Johnson's *Great Society* was the start of the *great dependency* on the federal government.

Aid to Families with Dependent Children. Sounds charitable. However, welfare was given to women as long as they weren't married. I have heard many people claim that there wasn't anyway someone would keep popping out babies just so they wouldn't have to work. "There isn't enough money in welfare to have a woman and her children live comfortably. Don't you think they would want to work if they could rather than collect a measly stipend?"

Side Note: You must have missed all the people voting for the candidate offering free stuff. Who wouldn't want free stuff? Wouldn't you love to shop, have lunch with the girls, golf, go out to eat, garden, sun yourself on a beach, then walk to your mailbox and pick up your monthly stipend from Uncle Sam?

Well, the proof is in the numbers. More out-of-wedlock births, numerous kids by different fathers. Then the daughters pop out babies and still lives with mom and that can calculate to a nice tidy sum. I know I wouldn't want to live that way. The money still keeps flowing, though, even when the woman does work. It has been reported there are women who turn down a promotion because it would put them over the threshold of earnings and they would lose out on $30,000+ in government subsidies. And it's still seared in my brain the image of the pot smoking surfer dude out in Hawaii collecting over $60,000 in welfare, shopping for lobster, living on the beach, playing his guitar, all at the taxpayers' expense. Some say there will always be some people who abuse the system, but we just have to look at those it helps. No. We have to root out the abusers who are bleeding the system of money needed for those who truly qualify.

Now the women popping out babies, the government should limit welfare payments to two children and that's it. Any amount over the limit and those baby daddies better cough up some dough or have one of them *put a ring on it* cause sucking on the government tit has to come to an end. During LBJ's reign, less than 10 percent of children grew up in a single parent household. Today, it has jumped to 33 percent. Back then less than 5 percent of babies were born to unmarried women. Today, it's 40 percent.

One only has to look at the history of the Plymouth Colony to see how colonists overcame hardships. The settlers brought socialism to America. That's all they knew. There was a communal garden and a communal storehouse for the crops. Crops were planted and each person was allowed so much of the yield whether they worked or not. Unfortunately, little by little fewer people showed up to do the planting and harvesting and some resorted to stealing. Starvation started to kill them off in numbers. Governor William Bradford decided to divide up the land and give each family a parcel. Whatever they grew and harvested, they kept for their own family. The colonists soon started to trade their crops, wares, fish, etc., with each other and the Natives. Thus was the beginning of free trade.

How did we lose our desire for self sufficiency and desire to accomplish something? Have we been influenced by our lay-about neighbors or family members? Has the government instilled a Big Brother mentality in our citizens? Do we look at those wanting the government to help them in every phase of their lives and think, "where's mine?" Can a society survive with a socialist mindset? In the words of Margaret Thatcher, "The problem with socialism is, sooner or later you run out of everyone else's money."

Side Note #1: Some people love to say Social Security is just another form of welfare. But, no, it isn't. People have [should] paid into it. See the Social Security section to find out how those who haven't put into it are aiding in sucking it dry.

Side Note #2: I always hear people say that the war on drugs isn't working so we should abolish it. Well, the war on poverty certainly isn't working. Should we abolish it? Some people definitely need a safety net but after $20 trillion, don't you think we should come up with a more cost-saving plan?

Course, one does wonder if there really are that many people living in what is considered poverty level. Many of the poor have cell phones, Internet, air conditioning, and many other conveniences. Almost half own their own home. Could it be the figures are inflated just so the boys in Washington can ask for more money to *end poverty*?

Just asking.

RACE RELATIONS

I, along with, I'm sure, millions of people, had high hopes with the election of the first black president. Boy, we have come so far. Boy, aren't we diverse. We can finally bury the racism and cynicism. How's that working out for us now? I don't think we have ever been more divided. No matter how much we want to pat ourselves on the back that we are an integrated country, we really aren't. And that's because people self-segregate. You hang out with people with a similar background, likes and dislikes, where you feel comfortable. I just read an article in a sports magazine on women golfers and it mentioned that the Korean women tend to eat together, travel together, stick together. It's human nature.

Chicago has its Chinatown. The south side of Chicago used to be all Italian. It slowly morphed to Serbian, and then Hispanic. The suburb my grandparents lived in was mainly Polish. There were two Catholic churches and in one of the churches Sunday masses were said only in Polish. We had a Polish deli. Gary used to be white, then it slowly changed. Once gangs and the drug business infiltrated, people fled for safety. Those who couldn't afford to move had to try to deal with the crime rate. Some call it white flight but it's actually survival. Once gangs start tagging garages, homeowners don't want their houses to devalue so they sell as fast as possible. Is it right? Right for whom? If you have children, you think of their safety first. Even the mall where I used to live has a poor excuse for security. Guards weren't allowed to carry guns and shop owners were instructed to look the other way when a theft was taking place.

Is this a way to live? Is this how you teach consequences to actions? I don't think any family, no matter the ethnicity, wants to live or raise a family in that kind of environment. The mayors and city fathers need to take control. There has to be a better police presence, although how can you blame them for being apprehensive? Police and even firefighters have been targeted when they answer a call.

It all starts at the top, and that's with our Commander in Chief. The left claims stricter gun laws are needed. Some cities, like Chicago, have some of the strictest gun laws yet it has one of the highest incidence of shootings. Instead, how about stricter penalties? A slap on the wrist doesn't cut it anymore. Residents are terrified to testify or report anything they have witnessed. There are others, though, who don't want to help. I remember walking out of a Dunkin' Donuts one day and seeing a couple in front of me wearing tee shirts that read, "Don't be a snitch." Really? Why not? If you see something, say something. Yes, fear of reprisal factors in, but don't say there aren't others who want to protect *their own* and don't want to help the police one bit.

I don't think there is one person who can say we haven't come a long way from the Civil Rights era. There are people and organizations who like nothing better than to fuel distrust and hatred. I personally believe the majority of people only want to live their lives in peace, provide for their families, feel accepted, and not disregarded.

This is where I think things went sideways. History can tell you (although one never knows how much History is taught in schools these days), how disregarded and slighted certain ethnicities were treated in the past. Whether black, Irish, Japanese, Native American…even women, people were treated differently. Those who were laborers, whether slaves or women, were made to feel far beneath those in higher *stations*. Was this a carry-over from Mother England where royalty was far above the peasants ala *Downton Abbey*? Those highly educated looked down their noses at those who couldn't read or write?

Washington is now Downton Abbey and the voters (peasants) are the ones scrambling for the scraps tossed over the White House castle walls. When one group of peasants gets something the other groups don't, all hell breaks loose. Favoritism is the gasoline that fuels the fire of resentment. This Administration has been doling out goodies to everyone but U.S. citizens.

A $750 million package to some countries in South America to fight poverty, gang violence, and to help reform governments. (Thought we weren't in the nation building business anymore!) All this while we have poverty in various cities throughout the U.S., including homeless. And gang violence? When's the last time POTUS visited Chicago?

Obamacare calls for provisions for sex change operations while our veterans have trouble getting help for PTSD.

Christmas carols are prohibited while another religious group gets foot basins in colleges for washing their feet.

Just recently the U.S. pledged $770 billion to rebuild mosques in the Middle East while some of our cities, schools, roads, and bridges are crumbling. (Still waiting for those shovel ready jobs we were promised in 2009.)

You get the picture. Most are in the name of political correctness.

Washington can't make everyone happy, but when efforts are made to blatantly favor one group over the other, resentment builds.

Which brings me to…

IMMIGRATION

We have had immigration laws on the books since the 1800s. There have been a number of changes and amendments since then.

I did mention they are here illegally, right? Yet some people found the term *illegal alien* to have a negative connotation, so last March the Library of Congress decided to strike the term from its catalogs. They preferred *noncitizen* and *unauthorized immigrant*. I agree that the term *alien* does sound more like ET. However, if you enter a country illegally, you are illegal, right? Now Republicans approved a plan to require the LOC to change the term to *illegal immigrant*. Each side gets what it wants. Who says they can't work together?

The government has drawn a fine line between illegal immigrant and refugee. If you are fleeing some country in South America because of drug wars or government oppression, you aren't considered an illegal immigrant. And you receive all kinds of goodies: Medicaid, food stamps, cash, housing, SSI, education, around 80 different types of programs all at the U.S. taxpayers' expense. There are time limits on certain programs for us (U.S. citizens), but some of these same programs for a refugee can last their entire life. Thought in the olden days, like when my grandfather came here from Poland, you had to have a sponsor family here to provide a bed and monetary assistance until you got on your feet. What happened to that? And immigrants would be quarantined for a time to make sure they didn't have any health concerns. Certainly not being done today. The TB rate in Minnesota used to hover around 4%. Now with the influx of refugees in that state, the rate is up to 28%.

Our immigration program costs us close to $113 billion a year. State budgets are squeezed tight, especially those close to the border. But when it comes to refugees from the Middle East countries, our government doesn't even give states a heads up before relocating the refugees. Our President wants to relocate 10,000 refugees by the end of September, many from Syria. According to the Center for Immigration Studies, this will cost us $644 million over the course of five years. And, need I remind you, refugees are eligible for a boatload of welfare benefits.

And then there's the 14th Amendment which grants citizenship to anyone born or naturalized in the U.S. Unintended consequences. In 2015 authorities were closing down, what was termed *maternity tourism hotels*, in Los Angeles. Seems many wealthy Asian women were flying to the U.S. to have their babies, then flying home. Someone was making money in the *anchor baby* industry. Entrepreneurship. Gotta love it!

To be truthful, we need to query farmers, restaurants, hotels, and other employers of legal immigrants and determine exactly how many work visas can be issued. I don't think they have increased the number in decades. That has to change. This way we know who is coming into the country and for how long. And we will be able to screen them better. And the powers that be need to remember that some companies are starting to replace workers with robots and even some fast food restaurants are having customers use kiosks for ordering, thus cutting down on the number of employees. We already have too many workers and not enough jobs. (Another reason people should be encouraged to retire early!)

When my relatives came to the U.S., they had to be quarantined for a while and checked out for any known and unknown diseases. Today, all of the air travel makes it almost impossible to know what bug anyone is carrying. However, when they are coming over the border, welcome wagon or not, I don't hear of any physical exams taking place. Some diseases which have become almost non-existent in the U.S.—polio, measles, mumps, TB—are now making a comeback. You can imagine the strain on health facilities along the border and in towns where illegals and refugees are being placed. Yes, it's a good thing we have the medicines to combat these diseases, but wouldn't it be better to know who has what when they enter the country?

Which brings us to…

HEALTHCARE

No one should have to hold a fund raiser to pay off their hospital bills. Those with the means have no problem getting the best of care for themselves and their loved ones. Unfortunately, the Affordable Care Act is a disaster. "We have to pass the bill in order to find out what's in it." Really, Congress? If it is such a wonderful plan, why didn't every member of Congress, including the current occupant of the White House and his family, sign on to this wonderful insurance?

Yes, something needs to be done. I would like to have seen a study on different plans used in other countries. Let's hear about England, Switzerland, Denmark, Sweden, Canada, etc. How are these funded? High taxes? A VAT tax? What is it costing each citizen? What does each plan cover? Let's hear about those waiting lists, all the negatives as well as the positives. I want committee members who won't sugarcoat the findings. Then let these knowledgeable people propose how something like those plans would be funded here. Would we institute a VAT tax? Would the government handle it? (God help us!) Medicare is already sending doctors running from their practices. I have seen my doctor's bill and then what Medicare feels his services are worth. I wouldn't even work for those wages. We will all end up with doctors who only completed two years of medical school in Venezuela and can't speak English.

In a capitalist society, the government can't dictate how much doctors should be paid. One wonders if there shouldn't there be some type of regulation, though. Should a hospital be able to charge an exorbitant fee for a room? Who suffers if the government dictates a maximum amount? Does that mean the hospital cuts down from five night nurses to two? Or pays nurses half of what they are worth? How is that controlled without the government stepping in?

Some say we should allow the purchase of insurance over state lines. Would it really create more competition and lower costs? If so, by how much? Insurance needs to be portable and pre-existing conditions must be covered.

And let's not stop at healthcare. Dental and eye care are all part of our health. You can't be your healthiest if you don't have all of your teeth or healthy gums. I'm not saying everyone should have dental implants or eight pair of designer prescription lenses. With all the increases in the cost of healthcare services, for some reason, the maximum amount covered for dental services hasn't increased in over 50 years. Why? Certainly getting a filling or X-ray is less expensive than a hip X-ray or stitching up a cut in the ER, but over the years dental costs have increased. So what gives?

We want an insurance plan that is portable, insurance companies can sell anywhere in the U.S., pre-existing conditions need to be covered, and insurance levels should be offered. Say someone only wants to pay for catastrophic illness, which might be at a premium level, but all those minor visits to the doctor would be out-of-pocket. That would be one category. Single people who feel they are immune from all illnesses big and small, might/should opt for this category. After all, one texting while driving accident will make them wish they had catastrophic insurance. Which begs the question: If someone doesn't have catastrophic insurance and ends up in the hospital for weeks after such an accident, then what? I could say, "too bad," but won't. That's where the planners need to get into the weeds. Catastrophic insurance for family, individuals, a combined 80/20 with catastrophic....you get the picture.

But there's still the problem of insurance companies jacking up their prices, especially if there is a large pool of terminally ill patients. With all that those patients are going through, the last thing they need to worry about is a six-figure doctor and hospital bill. Health insurance is getting to be like car insurance: They like to receive your money but god help you if they are forced to pay it out.

So the panel has its work cut out for it: Bring in representatives or those knowledgeable of other countries' plans and lay out the facts. Have the Congressional Budget Office crunch the numbers and offer up the horror stories. (I will dismiss any mention of covering everyone with Medicare since that would require a vast addition of manpower to execute and oversight to make sure doctors and hospitals are paid in a timely manner and that no one is gouging the system.) Also, all of these committee meetings and panel discussions need to be televised so we know exactly what is being said and who is being interviewed. No more behind closed door meetings. The panel needs to devise the different plans insurance companies should adhere to, i.e., the single, family, 80/20, catastrophic, and let's not forget elderly care. I won't go into nursing home horror stories. Some are deplorable. Maybe we should leave them all in the care of Sisters of the Poor. When profit-making companies are in charge, some will find all kinds of ways to cut staff, cut their hours, and you know it's the patients who suffer. This isn't rocket science. If we can send a man to the moon, why can't we put together a healthcare program that is affordable and humane?

I know this has been bounced around before — how about taxing Internet sales? According to the Commerce Department, web sales in 2014 totaled close to $305 billion. I know some states have imposed taxes on Internet sales. Do we want to hit the consumer again with a federal tax? Would even one percent, or $3 billion, make a dent in the dollars needed for healthcare? Hardly. (But I bet if we add up all of the pork spending over the years we could have made a huge dent.)

Side Note: With how Obamacare is unraveling, one wonders if this was the plan all along. Make it so unworkable that we throw our hands up and scream, single-payer please!

ISIS/TALIBAN/FANATICS/TERRORISM

Not much to say here. The Middle East turns a blind eye, the United Nations gives a collective sigh, and there we are expending blood and money...for what? Why haven't there been any more videos of beheadings? Did ISIS tire of it? Whenever any video is shown of ISIS training camps or groups of them hunkered behind huge boulders in a sea of sand, I just have one question—Where do they get their food? I don't see a McDonald's nor do I see tailgating parties. Is there a large grill set up somewhere? Do they shoot for one hour then traipse back to the local drive-thru?

And what's with the young people flocking to their cause? In a way, it's not hard to understand. Serial killers receive fan mail. The Menendez brothers received marriage proposals...both are actually married now, but still serving life sentences. At the risk of sounding like an isolationist, we need to worry about the potential dangers within our own borders. Although the President has claimed that "we don't have a terrorist problem here, that Muslims have assimilated, there aren't any Muslim-only enclaves like they have in France and England," he obviously hasn't been to cities where even street signs have been changed to uncommon names. Powers that be claim these enclaves don't have their own courts or practice Sharia law, but how do we know if police are not allowed to enter? I have no problem with different religions having their own churches and synagogues, but if any part of any religion violates our laws, should we look the other way? Don't think so.

Yes, we have many different nationalities and religions in the U.S. We can't celebrate them all. We can't allow foot washing basins in every school any more than we can add communion wafers on the school menus. I know this is difficult for some people to understand, but we are a Christian nation. We speak English and everyone should learn English. We can't allow every school to recognize every holiday for every ethnic culture. Schools would be closed 300 days a year. Some would say we should recognize all or none. Sorry, that isn't how it works. You don't immigrate to the U.S. and then try to change our language, culture, and customs. You are here to become Americans, not make us conform to your way of life. We can accept your differences, welcome you into our schools and neighborhoods, share a meal and learn about your culture, but don't demand we change our language, holidays, court system, or even our political system. Just because in your country you are allowed to practice honor killings, here in America it's still called murder.

And, no, I'm not forgetting terrorism within our borders. Who can forget after 9/11? What I don't understand is why this Administration REFUSES to say the words *Islamic Extremism*. I had an *uh oh* moment when POTUS made a bowing gesture when meeting the Saudi King. WTF? His handlers tried to walk it back with some lame excuse. May as well say the king is shorter and POTUS was just trying to meet him at eye level.

We failed to connect the dots when the 9/11 terrorists were taking flying lessons, I mean take off lessons. No need to learn to land a plane.

In San Bernardino, neighbors said they were suspicious but didn't want to be labeled racist so kept quiet.

All kinds of dots were there ripe for connecting regarding the shooter at a nightclub in Orlando recently. A former co-worker saw and heard the racist comments. The FBI had interviewed the shooter a couple times a few years prior. We are too PC to s*ee something/say something.* Presidential candidates are quick to weigh in. One doesn't want us to rush to judgement, not label one religion because of one person's action, yet still unable to utter the words Islamic Extremism. The other candidate isn't one to coddle and has no problems calling it like it is, immediately being labeled dangerous. One side claims that hate is not being preached in certain mosques while the other side says we need to monitor them all.

How many more people have to die before we unleash the authorities to do what they have to do to keep us safe?

When will we learn?

PROTESTS

I grew up in the flower child era. However, I had zero interest in protesting. I was still in high school and had enough homework to keep me busy. For those who need a refresher course on our Constitution:

Amendment I.

Congress shall make no law respecting an establishment of religion, or prohibiting the free exercise thereof; or abridging the freedom of speech, or of the press, or the right of the people peaceably to assemble, and to petition the Government for a redress of grievances.

May I direct your attention to the phrase, *the right of the people PEACEABLY to assemble.* I don't see the words *set cars on fire, throw rocks at police, damage storefronts, loot and pillage.* The amount of damage, the cost to cities, business owners, homeowners, are never recouped.

Someone is applying the rules of Saul Alinsky quite well.

From *Rules for Radicals*:

***"An organizer must stir up dissatisfaction and discontent...** He must create a mechanism that can drain off the underlying guilt for having accepted the previous situation* *for so long a time. Out of this mechanism, a new community organization arises....*

"The job then is getting the people to move, to act, to participate; in short, to develop and harness the necessary ***power to effectively conflict with the prevailing patterns and change them****. When those prominent in the status quo turn and label you an 'agitator' they are completely correct, for that is, in one word,* ***your function—to agitate to the point of conflict.****"*

"Whenever possible, go outside the expertise of the enemy. *Look for ways to increase insecurity, anxiety and uncertainty.*

"Ridicule is man's most potent weapon. *It is almost impossible to counteract ridicule. Also it infuriates the opposition, which then reacts to your advantage."*

I have a wonderful suggestion. Many of these protests appear pretty well organized, like Black Lives Matter. Professional signs have been produced. The Occupy Wall Street people were prepared with tents, sleeping bags, change of clothes, food, not to mention they all appeared to know where and when to be wherever. Someone or some group is financially supporting these protests. After all, most have to get from Point A to Point B, sometimes by air. Some of these people appear to be professional protestors. All we need is to find the people and organizations footing the bill and charge them for any damages to property and injuries to people. There has to be a money trail somewhere and I assume these people have deep pockets. We need to hit them where it hurts. You have to obtain a parade permit in cities. Why not a protest permit and charge $1,000 per person? If the protest is peaceful, you refund part of the money. (I say part because of the trash these people leave and someone has to clean it up, right?) Anything other than that, the protestors and their financial supporters suffer the consequences.

Hey, tough love. It works!

Side Note: Please, when protesting X, Y, and Z, have the common decency to wave the <u>American</u> flag!

SOCIAL SECURITY

Ahhhh, the safety net for seniors. When originally enacted in 1935, the life expectancy for a man was 58, and a woman 62. However, eligible age to collect Social Security was 65. How clever of the politicians. Sure, some people lived beyond 58 and 62, but I don't think the architects of the program foresaw how the life expectancy figures would increase. Nor did they foresee added Amendments, like unemployment insurance, Aid to Families with Dependent Children, maternal and child welfare, public health services, and the blind. The administration was hoping it would encourage older workers to retire, thereby freeing up jobs for younger people. (Today, unfortunately, this would be called age discrimination.)

Interestingly, back then some states excluded children born out of wedlock. Today that would certainly discourage women from popping out five and six babies.

With all these added Amendments, do you think the powers that be even considered that they might possibly not have enough money? Here's some interesting tidbits from the Wikipedia website:

The first reported Social Security payment was to Ernest Ackerman, a Cleveland motorman who retired only one day after Social Security began. Five cents were withheld from his pay during that period, and he received a lump-sum payout of seventeen cents from Social Security.

The first monthly payment was issued on January 31, 1940 to Ida May Fullwer of Ludlow, Vermont. In 1937, 1938, and 1939, she paid a total of $24.75 into the Social Security System. Her first check was for $22.54. After her second check, Fuller already had received more than she contributed over the three-year period. She lived to be 100, and she collected a total of $22,888.92.

In 1940, benefits paid totaled $35 million. These rose to $961 million in 1950, $11.2 billion in 1960, $31.9 billion in 1970, $120.5 billion in 1980, and $247.8 billion in 1990 (all figures in nominal dollars, not adjusted for inflation). In 2004, $492 billion of benefits were paid to 47.5 million beneficiaries. In 2009, nearly 51 million Americans received $650 billion in Social Security benefits.

According to the U.S. Chamber of Commerce (2/29/16), our *safety net programs* (Social Security, Medicare, Medicaid), ate up 58 percent of the tax revenue at the turn of the century. By 2015 it grew to 78 percent. By 2026, mandatory programs will represent 99 percent of federal revenue.

How on earth does Washington expect Social Security to remain solvent? What used to be a contribution by workers to be paid to workers upon retirement, morphed to include children, those who never worked and never contributed, and even elderly immigrants. To add to the big sucking sound, women after a certain age can collect part of her husband's social security, even if she never worked, BUT it doesn't reduce his benefits at all. Congress did try to make adjustments, eventually raising the tax from the original 2%. But then Medicare and Medicaid were added to the program in 1965.

During the Johnson administration in 1968, the decision was made to dump the SS trust funds into the general budget, thereby giving them a golden goose of money they could spend on other things rather than raising taxes. Shouldn't Congress have been held accountable for raiding the trust fund? Why does everyone now have to suffer as Congress raises taxes and changes retirement ages just to make up for the stolen money? Who said politicians weren't smart, or is that clever? They were even brave enough to make amendments during general election years because they were giving out goodies. But then reality bit them in the ass and the financial outlook revealed long-term deficits which threatened insolvency. At that point, amendments were made in odd numbered years (non-election years). Any type of Social Security changes could only mean tax increases and/or benefit reductions.

Social Security relies on high employment in order to generate enough revenue to remain solvent. Today we have at least 90 million people not working. Many of the new jobs today are low paying, which reduces the amount of SS withholdings. And there are those who are paid under the table so those contributions are non-existent. Then there are the baby boomers retiring at a record number. As though Johnson moving SS dollars into the general fund wasn't bad enough, under the Clinton administration a decision was made to tax Social Security. There must be something in our Constitution prohibiting the government from taxing a tax, wouldn't you think?

I hear another sucking sound — the Supplemental Security Income, which gives monetary assistance to the low income aged, blind, and disabled. Although it is claimed payments are NOT paid out of the Social Security program, you are directed to the Social Security website for information on SSI. This money supposedly is paid out of the U.S. Treasury general funds, not Social Security trust fund. But aren't all of these monies in the same fiscal pot? SSI replaces a federal-state adult assistance program, a program which obviously obtained its funding from somewhere else, so we are to believe it isn't depleting any part of Social Security.

There are kids who, if a parent reaches the age of 65, each child starts to collect a Social Security check until age 18, even though the parent is still alive, and even though it doesn't decrease the parent's benefits.

And who else is a recipient? Immigrants and refugees. How solvent are these funds now that the administration has placed a *Welcome* sign on our borders?

Just asking.

Contrary to public belief, not all seniors live high on the hog. Almost 50% of seniors live in poverty. I call this a ***War on Seniors***!

Many live on modest savings, meager pensions, and whatever Social Security they are entitled to. Some living in retirement communities are living SS check to SS check. They may have purchased a house fifty years ago for $12,000, sold it for $150,000, and used that money for their retirement home. Some even work part-time to make ends meet. For the past three years, retirees haven't received a cost of living increase in their Social Security benefits yet the cost of food, medicine, and doctor bills has gone up. Congress has no problem giving themselves a raise.

How to fix Social Security. Some want to increase the threshold of taxable income for the wealthy. Some want to apply the 6.2% tax onto the entire earnings of the wealthy. After all, how much money does Bill Gates need? But, is it fair? It would certainly help to make Social Security solvent for future generations. Once you start to reduce benefits or take away a portion of the program, everyone screams foul. Politicians don't want to touch any type of change, especially during an election year.

Next, we have the Americans with Disability Act. Which department(s) does this fall under? It's important that the disabled receive some type of funding. However, let's tighten up those qualifications a bit. Rules changed under this Administration. All you need now is a hangnail, a case of depression or anxiety from losing a job, or some other inane excuse to qualify for benefits. The main reason this was done was so once the unemployment benefits ran out, the administration could move people to the disability trough and they wouldn't have to be factored into the unemployment rate. So let's cut those benefits off. Let's find money elsewhere to bulk up that department's budget and let them pay out the disability benefits rather than from the Social Security fund. I'm sure Congress can move money from shrimp on treadmills, stuttering mice, and the $500 million the Administration plans to give to the United Nations climate change program (which was somehow done WITHOUT obtaining congressional approval.)

This department would also have a more uniform way of determining a person's disability. Before you call me a heartless witch, anyone abusing the system is taking away money from those who truly need it. Unless we start to scrutinize every application more closely, there will be a continual drain of our resources.

Why on earth do we pay a portion of a husband's Social Security benefits to a wife who is <u>still working</u> and earning a pay check, yet we don't reduce the husband's future benefits at all? Can someone explain this to me? Isn't this a bit like double-dipping? And I don't think the wife's future Social

Security benefits are reduced in any way either. So what gives?

Now politicians are talking about raising the age to 70 to qualify for Social Security since the life expectancy age has risen. Do they really think there are that many jobs out there for 70 year olds? How many bagger jobs at Walmart are available? If we can get seniors out of the work force at 66, doesn't that free up jobs for college graduates?

How would politicians feel if we decreased their benefits? Made them work until they were 70? Oh, wait. They already do. Some have to be wheeled in to vote on a bill. I say there should be an age limit, 65 would be good, or as soon as they are unable to speak a coherent sentence.

As mentioned before, there should be a class in middle and high school on finance and investments. They should no longer rely on Social Security to be there when they retire. It may be there, but may only be a portion of what current retirees are receiving.

Move Social Security out of the General Fund, stop taxing Social Security, move the funding of SS Disability, Supplemental Security Income and any other non-applicable funding, OUT of the Social Security account. How would Congressional members like it if their pension money was dumped into the General Fund to be spent, leaving I.O.U slips of paper in its place?

Just saying.

POLITICAL CORRECTNESS

Enough already with the PC culture. My head is about to explode. It's obvious just about everyone can say they are offended by something said, written, displayed, manufactured, ad nauseum. Where's Archie Bunker when you need him? Oh, for the good old days when people could take a bit of ribbing or a joke without calling the ACLU. Even Mother Goose stories aren't fun anymore. There was no such thing as political correctness when I was growing up. I don't even remember any mention before 1990. What the hell happened? Did I wake up in Wayward Pines instead of America? It wasn't overnight. I think it has been slowly creeping into our lives, a manufactured label on behavior.

This reminds me of the movie, *Demolition Man*. It was a great look into a future where criminals were frozen rather than executed, where a czar governed by regulations and dictated what people could say and eat. Handshaking, kissing or intermingling of body fluids weren't allowed. Even songs on the radio were sanitized. No one was armed, not even the police. All of the weapons used in bygone eras were housed in a museum. Then a criminal played by Wesley Snipes is thawed, breaks into the museum, and goes on a killing rampage. A cop, Sylvester Stallone, also frozen for getting hostages killed in a standoff, has to be thawed because he is the only one who can stop Snipes. Sometimes that's how I feel. Someone woke me from a deep freeze and dumped me into a time warp I don't recognize. Is it too much to ask that people shrug into some thick skin? Can we have a little reality here? How about a little common sense?

Which brings us to…

So a school district in Illinois gets into hot water because they wouldn't allow a transgender student who identifies himself as female to shower in the girls' locker room. Really?! What happened to a right to privacy? I didn't even like showering with females when I was in high school so to let someone gain access whose *equipment* isn't the same as a female's is ludicrous.

As if schools don't have enough problems with students beating up teachers as well as each other or shooting up schools, what the administration is more concerned about, it appears, is to make sure any transgender student is allowed to use the bathroom according to the gender he/she feels he is, not the gender he was born. The U.S. Justice Department dangles a 2014 Title IX federal law prohibiting sex-based discrimination as their premise for bullying schools to adhere if they don't want federal funding withheld.

Perhaps kids are more in tune with their bodies these days, or perhaps there is too much focus on sex than in my day. All I know is that I didn't care for boys until I was in high school. It didn't mean at the age of ten that I thought I was a lesbian. I didn't even know what that word meant. We didn't have sex education in our schools (and gee, our pregnancy rate was practically non-existent). Today movies, magazines, ads, television programs…heck, even TV commercials are laced with sexual innuendo. This doesn't in anyway mean I have little sympathy for any teen with conflicting emotions. But don't we have this backwards? If one kid is allergic to peanuts, rather than have him eat lunch in the teachers' lounge, they prohibit all kids from bringing peanut butter sandwiches to school. With the bathroom issue, rather than have the transgender student use the teachers' lounge, they force all of the students into an uncomfortable situation.

If it was just using a bathroom, do the unisex bathrooms ala the former TV show, *Ally McBeal*. But using the showers in the girls (or boys) locker room? At some point, basic common sense has to prevail, especially with teens and raging hormones.

And then there are the adults…

Several years ago my husband and I were sitting at a bar when a *questionable* female pulled up a stool next to me. I first noticed the hairy knuckles, then the five o-clock shadow. He was dressed nice. Damn, even I couldn't maneuver on those four-inch heels. But then he got up to go to the bathroom and dammit if he didn't go to the women's room. I hooked a gaze in the bartender's direction, and she shook her head. "He comes in here at least once a week. I've never seen him use the women's bathroom before," she said. Then she headed to the manager's office. It may not be PC in some people's minds, but there isn't any way I am using a bathroom with a guy. Do you want to use the same facilities as a guy who had burritos for breakfast? Not gonna happen!

Another one that raises my blood pressure is a video on *White Guilt* playing at a neighborhood high school near you. It shows students at a starting line. The white kids get a head start and are around the track one time before they let the minorities start. Then obstacles are tossed in the minorities' way along the track. The main thing wrong with this scenario is affirmative action. For years minorities and women have been accepted into colleges and/or granted scholarships before the white male, even those with higher SAT scores. If anything, they should have the minorities and women having a one lap head start before the white guys. Another effort at brainwashing our kids.

Just my opinion.

There are certain people whose entire existence is based on promoting victimhood. What ever happened to Martin Luther King's character over skin color? We aren't in the 1960s anymore. We need kids to focus on the opportunities available to them that were never available fifty years ago.

Is your blood pressure up yet?

Schools are not allowed to give out an aspirin to a student without a parent's permission. Now a San Francisco middle school wants to give out condoms to students without telling the parents. Where on earth is our society headed? Better question, what is with San Francisco? It is so far left it is going to fall right into the Pacific. I will hold out hope that parents have an uprising soon.

Oh, it gets better!

A group of middle school kids found a book in the school library titled, *It's Perfectly Normal*. There were illustrations in the book showing naked teens and adults, some depicting sex acts and even masturbation. School officials tried to explain it away that it was meant for students ages 10 (10??) and up and was on some state approved list of books okay for schools. The officials claimed the book was accidentally left out by a sixth grade class and said it was an honest mistake. So age 12 is better than 10?

Much to their credit, parents were in an uproar. But really, besides needing a watch group to oversee what school officials are doing, who watches the department that makes up the list of approved books? I'm sure there are people who will say kids see and read much worse on their cell phone or their computers. Just because they can, doesn't mean they should.

One college (had to be the East Coast) sent out a directive

instructing students on avoiding offensive Halloween costumes. I think my head really did explode. As if that wasn't laughable enough, now colleges are instituting safe spaces. Like, what? A room filled with bouncing balls so they don't fall and hurt themselves? Not likely. These are spaces on campus set aside to insulate the little darlings from speech that may hurt their sensitivities.

Just when you thought you had heard it all! But…read on!

Have you heard of manspreading? Leave it up to California to recognize a massive problem that needs the government's attention. Men are sitting on buses and subway seats as though their legs had been permanently realigned after spending one month riding an elephant. They just can't seem to put their legs closer together, leaving other passengers to stand while the ingrate takes up two spaces. California's decision is to have a strict one ticket, one seat policy. This epidemic is spreading to other states. Here come the fines—$100 for the first offense, $200 for the second within a 12 month period. After that there will be a $500 fine for each repeat offense within five years. Will bus drivers hand out tickets? Will there be a manspread meter maid onboard? Or do the fellow riders get to take pictures with their cell phones to send to the police, TV stations, or social media? Stay tuned.

So how did all this start?

Webster's definition of political correctness: *agreeing with the idea that people should be careful to not use language or behave in a way that could offend a particular group of people.*

Dummy me thought political correctness was a relatively new term, maybe 20 years old. When trolling through the library and the Internet, I found a number of differing opinions. Some think it's an offspring of the Sixties' *if it feels good do it* era. Others believe it started after World War I and has its roots in Marxism. That should have had the garlic and crucifix at the ready. Cultural Marxism IS political correctness, identifying victim groups, whether it's oppressing women, homosexual rights, blacks, Hispanics, fill in the blanks. Majority of opinions point to college campuses where this mindset is cultivated and nurtured. (Someone once said, *whoever controls the children, controls our future.*) Young zombie minds are ripe for cultivation.

It starts even sooner than college. I read somewhere that a sixth grade teacher advised a student to tell her parents they are invading her privacy if they look at her emails or Facebook page. So much for parental authority. Students trust their teachers. After all, some spend more time with their teachers in a day than their parents.

Back to the Marxists who believed the main problem with society was Western civilization. After World War II it's believed some of these Marxist followers fled to the U.S.

and cloaked their beliefs in the term critical theory (aka destructive criticism). This is evident in the terms we hear today: homophobe, war on women, Islamophobe, racist, bigot, any critical term which immediately puts someone on the defensive. It even spills over into Nature and the Climate Change fanatics. If you don't agree, you are a denier, with the Department of Justice threatening to make it a crime to deny the existence of climate change.

Somehow Freud figures into all of this with his theory that all inhibitions and obsessions were the result of sexual repression. That's where we get into the *if it feels good, do it* Sixties anti-war protestors and flower children. So Hollywood trots out movies and television shows that keep pushing the envelope. Playboy and Hustler get even more brazen. Drugs run rampant and society rings its hands… well, half of society. One side is counting its money, the other side is wondering where the heck we are headed and how did it happen?

Some scholars believe this trail of PC crumbs started in 1916 and grows steadily today. (Jeez, these people are certainly patient.) The 1st Amendment is tossed out the window on college campuses as over 300 speakers are uninvited because some students don't like what the speaker stands for. (One college is providing three months of therapy sessions for students traumatized after a political candidate's speech.)

It spills over into our daily lives, in schools and business offices where we now have sensitivity training and Departments of Diversity and Inclusion. Movements have been started to erase offensive words, such as names of sports teams.

(Side bar: In a recent poll, 90% of Native Americans have zero problems with the name Washington Redskins.)

Playgrounds have stopped games we loved when I was growing up, like tag and red rover. We now have grief counselors in schools, as if parents are no longer needed to support and assist their own children. Some schools have done away with Valedictorians and Honor Society because not everyone can be picked so feelings will be hurt. (A recent headline in the news reported that a North Carolina school board voted to drop valedictorians because they believe it created unhealthy competition among students.) Since when is competition unhealthy? What's next…eliminate spelling bees?

One professor claims that our language would run too freely without political correctness to rein it in.

Cities and schools change the term Christmas to Holiday and avoid the words Baby Jesus and Santa Clause, lest anyone not Christian be offended. A New York city school principal banned Thanksgiving, the pledge, and Santa.

Officials feel the terms *convict* and *felon* are stigmatizing so the Department of Justice is replacing them with *person who was incarcerated* or *person who committed a crime*.

You definitely can't make this stuff up.

P. Atkinson wrote in ***A Study of our Decline***: *Unless plain speaking is allowed, clear thinking is denied. There can be no good reason for denying freedom of expression, there is no case to rebut, only the empty slogans of people inspired by selfishness and unrestrained by morality. The proponents of this nonsense neither understand the implications of what they say, nor why they are saying it: they are insane; which must mean that any community that embraces Political Correctness has discarded sanity.*

'Nuff said.

MISCELLANEOUS RANTS

Where's the Truth?

Why are manufacturers allowed to "stretch the truth" in advertising? Why are they allowed to use models wearing false eyelashes? Skin lotion will make me look ten years younger? Stop using 20-year-old models on anti-aging commercials. And car ads where the car is speeding at one hundred miles an hour? Have they tried maneuvering the Dan Ryan expressway during rush hour? And let's not forget the burgers and sub sandwiches that are piled four inches high, but when you buy it you can barely find the meat. Regulate this, Washington!

Don't Do As I Say…Do As I Do

Why is it when some people turn vegan or gluten free (or fill-in-the-blank) they are compelled to force everyone else to do the same? Follow whatever fad you want but leave the rest of us out of it.

Example of Too Much Money?

The University of New Hampshire spent $17,000 on a custom-made chef's table for the campus dining hall. Huh?

Richest or Debtest?

Why does the media and powers that be keep referring to the U.S. as the *richest nation*? A rich nation is NOT $20 trillion in debt.

When they say redistribution of wealth, is their intention to make other nations rich or to make the U.S. poorer?

The Grass is Always Greener

For those who claim to love Socialism or Communism, why do they put themselves through so much angst living in a capitalist country? Why don't they move to Venezuela or Russia where they can be happier rather than trying to change us?

Slap 'em Where it Hurts…Then Slap Harder

One thing that really bugs me is litter. I know we can't have a cop on every corner, but I wish we could have a camera on every street, highway, and parking lot. People are absolute pigs. And they do it because they are 99 percent sure they won't get caught. What we need are huge fines. The heck with having a penalty fit the crime. If you want a deterrent, slap them where it hurts. I say $1,000 for the first offense and add $1,000 for every offense after. And, give them a stretch of street or highway to clean once a week. Then they can see firsthand what an eyesore it is and what messy pigs some people are. Just once I would like to see a judge toss a lawyer out of the courtroom who wants to argue that the defendant is innocent, that the wind blew existing garbage off the street and made it look like he tossed it out. Make the lawyer join his client cleaning up the roadside. That judge would have my vote. Matter of fact, those idiots that run a red light? How about a $5,000 fine? That would have Speedy Gonzales slamming his foot on the brake pedal rather than the gas. Naturally, there are those who want to coddle the offender, give him/her a slap on the wrist. Paint those of us who are tired of the coddling as old meanies.

Made Where?

I don't know about you but I am sick and tired of not seeing "Made in the USA" on products in the store. I know global trade is good, but don't we make anything here anymore? Does the cost of labor end up pricing a shirt at $90? Why should it? Is there some hidden trade deal with China we don't know about, like they loan us money so we have to buy everything from them? I remember owning towels for ten years before they started to fray. Now I'm lucky they last through two washings. I say if a company sends defective products, we fine them. Is that too much to ask? And why are our harbors loaded with hundreds of thousands of shipping containers? Are the trade deals so one-sided that we aren't permitted to export anything? Who on earth negotiated that deal?

The Berry Amendment was enacted in 1941 and requires military clothing, tents, tarps, etc., be produced in the USA. So why are our military recruits still wearing athletic shoes NOT made here?

For English Press…..

Grrrrrrrrr. Okay, we have a lot of different languages spoken in this country. My grandparents were Polish. Gram's English was very broken. Gramp's was a bit better. But at least they learned English. To be fair, we can only pick one. Either that or we would be on the phone for an hour while the robot assigned a number to each language. There are close to 350 different languages spoken in the U.S. and I'm immediately hit with Spanish. Why not Polish? Vietnamese? French? How can you help immigrants learn English if you give them the alternative of not bothering to learn? And while I'm on the subject, you have to be a citizen to vote. So why are there ballots in Spanish?

If you are going to give immigrants a drivers license, they have to know English in order to read the road signs. Right? Do you want to be on the road, or even crossing a street, with drivers who have no idea what the signs say or mean?

Just asking.

Reading, Writing, and…Tripping?

What is it with kids and curiosity? At what point does that part of their brain mature? If experts say not until they are 25 or 30, what on earth are they doing in a voting booth at 18? But I digress. Now these bored kiddies thought it might be cool to eat flower seeds. Seems someone told them they can get high on certain seeds, but their curiosity landed them in an emergency room. Do seed manufacturers now have to have warning labels on their seed packets?

California Dreamin'

Course, you gotta step over all the homeless first. Pull up a piece of concrete and settle in. I know, I know, some are mentally ill. So why aren't they in a clinic or hospital where they can get the help they need? Oh, I forgot. Authorities can't force anyone to be committed. Finger pointing goes from politicians to psychiatrists to Libertarian lawyers. (Need I repeat?—Unintended consequences!) Then we have military veterans, many of whom also aren't getting the medical attention they need. However, there are alcoholics and drug addicts doing big potty in front of businesses, shooting up in front of kids on their way to school. Is that the impression city fathers want tourists to have? And here's a state with some of the highest taxes yet they are broke. Maybe they should look at exactly where the welfare money is being spent as they pat themselves on the backs for having sanctuary cities.

You Want to See My What?

Yes, we want to (or should want to) see your drivers license or picture I.D. when you vote. Shouldn't be that hard. Other countries do it. You need I.D. to purchase adult beverages, cigarettes, a gun, airline ticket, cell phone, certain cold medicines, rent an apartment, rent a hotel room, apply for a fishing or hunting license, apply for unemployment, food stamps, welfare…and the list goes on.

What's That Sucking Sound?

We taxpayers are a benevolent group, aren't we? A new regulation from the Department of Health and Human Services mandates that health insurers cover sex change operations subsidized by taxpayers through Medicare, Medicaid, and Obamacare. This is under the Nondiscrimination in Health Programs and Activities.

And I can't even get dental or eye care covered under Medicare? Who exactly is being discriminated against? And according to this rule, providers cannot refuse to cover hormone therapy, breast implants, and the surgery itself. And I can't even get breast implants! Seniors, rise up! We are being discriminated against!

Lights, Cameras, Barf Bag

I believe it was the movie *Leaving Las Vegas* where we were first introduced to on-screen bodily functions. The camera showed a woman on the toilet. Guess we weren't shocked enough. Next came…

Sex, full blown naked bodies writhing and moaning. And it wasn't even pay per view!

Vomiting. I think…no, I know, I'd rather see the sex. Nothing worse than watching someone puke. And movie and television directors think this is engaging the viewers?

As if watching someone vomit isn't bad enough…

Do directors really think we love watching shaking, moving cameras ala *Blair Witch Project*? I will give a TV show two tries. If they tamp down the shaking camera by the second episode, I'll continue watching. If they continue it or it gets worse, that's it. I won't be watching the show anymore.

The Shepherd Has No Clothes

German Shepherd, that is. I say no more male dogs in commercials. Use only female dogs or male dogs with very long hair. I don't need to see Fido and all his doggie junk leaping for a Frisbee or charging to the food bowl. Either girl dogs or put some clothes on him!

Can We Get a Robe Here?

Why do men on the PGA tour have to wear shirts with collars and long pants, even in 90 degree heat, yet the LPGA can dress like they have a pole dancing job after their round of golf? Some of their skirts are so short they can barely bend over. Tops are so tight they can hardly breathe. No, I'm not jealous of young, shapely bodies. I just don't see why the men have to dress professionally and the women don't. Why can't the men wear shorts on hot days? Is the LPGA trying to attract more viewers (translation: more money) by providing eye candy for the male couch potatoes?

Just asking.

How Many Rubber Trees Does It Take to Make...

The Olympics are coming to Rio and what are they doing to prepare for it, other than killing a bunch of Zika mosquitos? Why, they are providing 450,000 condoms for distribution. That's three times more than they provided for the London Games. Pardon me, but I thought when athletes are in training, they avoid alcohol, tobacco, and other distractions. No, before you say it, I'm not a prude. I just know my priorities, if it were me.

Wonder how many babies will be born in May 2017?

Buddy Can You Spare a Dime or Dollar?

Economy is great you say? Hmmmmmm. New headline says that two-thirds of Americans would be hard-pressed today to come up with $1,000 if there were an emergency. I know I can't.

Still feel like we live in a rich Nation?

The Supremes

Why do the Supreme Court justices get lifetime tenure? I know it's in the Constitution; but in this year's battle for the White House, the replacement of Justice Scalia plays heavily. Why not some formula like 25 years of service or 65 years of age? What do we do when a Justice is noticeably mentally incapacitated? What would happen is some far left leaning Socialist were to be elected president and four Justices retired? Would the makeup of the Court truly represent the majority of the country? (See section on **Elections** regarding how only 25% to 30% of the country elects a president.)

Just asking (and shuddering!)

Pass the Salt, Pepper, and Another Gun Law, Please!

According to figures cited years ago, there are 20,000 various gun laws in the U.S. Some dispute that figure but can't come up with any other statistics. One thing I know for sure, cities with the strictest gun laws, like Chicago, have some of the worst gun violence.

What's the solution from the brainiacs? Pass another gun law. Here's a novel idea taken from the Swiss. How about, by law, every home HAS to have a gun? Gun registrations and gun safety classes are required, no assault weapons, and criminal records or mental illness ban you from ownership. (Those HIPPA privacy laws need to be given a common sense review.) Same law across all 50 states. No patchwork of laws, other than if a state wants to allow concealed carry. And yes, pass all the laws you want but people will still break them so toughen up the penalties.

For those still questioning why guns at all, this from the BBC News: Hermann Suter, vice-president of the Swiss lobbying group Pro Tell, says, "The gun at home is the best way to avoid dictatorships—only dictators take arms away from the citizens."

Check Lane Announcers

Can sports announcers, whether baseball, football, golf, et al, please stick to play-by-play action? Like headlines in the check lane gossip magazines, we, the viewers, have to hear how Joe Hockey's wife just had a birthday, Barry Fastball's mother just completed two years of cancer treatments, Tiger Fairway attended his high school reunion last night and still made his tee off time. If you want to fill dead space, play some music!

IN CONCLUSION

Is there really an end? As I write this I'm reading other headlines of waste and stupidity.

Grab a stiff one and read on...

One Pennsylvania high school yearbook included quotes from, of all people, Hitler, Stalin, and the ISIS leader.

A study from the Pew Research has found that more men and women between the ages of 18 and 34 are opting to live with mommy and daddy. (I would have changed the locks or moved the minute they left for college.) But the economy is good…chugging right along, right?

Anyone see a suitcase stuffed with $305 million lying around anywhere? That's how much the state of Oregon is missing. Seems the benevolent government (we, the taxpayers) gave Oregon that amount to set up the state healthcare exchanges. Never happened. And the investigation continues.

Haven't had enough PC? Almost drove off the road when I heard on the radio that some groups want to discourage people from asking childless couples, "Are you planning a family?" Guess it makes childless couples feel bad, inadequate, fill in the blank.

As you can tell, as I try to finish this book, more thoughts pop into my head, more inane headlines scream from the front pages. And if I keep reading headlines and watching the news, I'll never get this book published. So I will just keep a folder of notes and soon I should have enough for another book, provided, however, that you don't see my name in the Obits.

M.A. Wyner

M.A. Wyner is the author of numerous books under a variety of names. You can contact her at:

mawyner@sc.rr.com

www.ingramcontent.com/pod-product-compliance
Lightning Source LLC
Chambersburg PA
CBHW020659300426
44112CB00007B/442